Stories from the River of Mercy

Stories from the River of Mercy

The True Journey of Two Women Who Find Grace and Mercy in Deep Blue Waters

Sheila Walsh

A
JANET
THOMA
BOOK

THOMAS NELSON PUBLISHERS
Nashville

Published in Nashville, Tennessee, by Thomas Nelson, Inc.

Scripture quotations noted NKJV are from THE NEW KING JAMES VERSION. Copyright © 1979, 1980, 1982, Thomas Nelson, Inc., Publishers.

Scripture quotations noted NIV are from the HOLY BIBLE: NEW INTER-NATIONAL VERSION®. Copyright © 1973, 1978, 1984 by International Bible Society. Used by permission of Zondervan Publishing House. All rights reserved.

Library of Congress Cataloging-in-Publication Data

Miller, Sheila Walsh, 1956–
        Stories from the river of mercy : the true journey of two women who find grace and mercy in deep blue waters / Sheila Walsh.
            p. cm.
        Includes bibliographical references.
        ISBN 0-7852-6875-8
        1. Christian biography—United States. 2. Miller, Sheila Walsh, 1956– .
        3. Pfaehler, Eleanor. I. Title.

BR1725.M449 A3 2000
248.8'66'092—dc21   99-056247
    [B]   CIP

Printed in the United States of America

1 2 3 4 5 6 BVG 05 04 03 02 01 00

This book is dedicated to Christian Walsh Pfaehler by two women who love you very much, your mommy and your nana. We offer this story as a remembrance of the goodness of God in all the days of our lives. In our good days and in our bad days, we are loved with an everlasting love. Remember that, darling boy.

Contents

Acknowledgments

Janet, I want to thank you with all my heart for your vision and passion for this book. You stood by my side, encouraging me to tell this story. I believe this book will impact the lives of many families. Eleanor and I thank you.

*E*leanor at age nineteen.

Our Story

I never imagined I would write a book like this. To write about the relationship between two people when you are one of the two and the other one is gone, how could that ever be fair? How could my version of the events that changed our lives forever be the whole truth? I know now that I don't even remember all that happened.

What I do know is that when Eleanor Pfaehler and I met, we stood on opposite sides of an invisible, and seemingly insurmountable, wall. She was Barry Pfaehler's mother, and I was his girlfriend. Barry was an only child; Eleanor and William had waited twelve long years for this baby boy who now shared his heart and his dreams with me. Eleanor and I talked over this wall. At times we reached up to hug. But the wall was always there.

Then Eleanor was diagnosed with liver cancer. For a time the wall got higher. Finally, by the grace and mercy of God alone, that wall came crashing down. Eleanor and I found ourselves swimming in the river of mercy with our arms around each other, holding each other up, willing to give our lives for the other.

What happened? I'm not sure I understand it completely. All I know is that Eleanor found in her dying what she had been looking for in her living, and I got over myself enough to see beyond the stuff that doesn't matter to love my mother-in-law, my sister in Christ. The events that happened in the last few weeks of her life made me realize I could try to write this down, because in the end Eleanor trusted me in her most vulnerable, weak moments. She even gifted me with the care of her body, a most intimate, sacred charge.

Before we get there, however, I have to tell you where we began. It's not always pretty, but it's true. I find it strange that it seems so hard for us as Christians to tell the truth. I was in New York recently and a reporter asked me what one question I am asked more than any other. That was easy: "Do you find it hard to be so honest?"

Isn't that a strange question to ask a Christian? Apparently not. Lies are much more comfortable and comforting. We long to be inspiring—yet, the truth is, much of our everyday lives is not inspiring. For myself, I have made a new commitment to simply tell the truth.

I have been changed by Eleanor's life and death, as indeed she was. So this is our story. It's not my story. It's *our* story. I have included some of the psalms that I read to Eleanor in her last days. I have shared some of her favorite hymns so that you can join the worship service of our last days together. I have also included some song lyrics from my album *Blue Waters*, and other poems I wrote throughout this time.

So now, I like to think that she is sitting right beside me as I write. In a way she is. She is part of the fabric of my life forever. Only God could have done that.

Part One

In the Beginning

I am still confident of this:
I will see the goodness of the LORD
    in the land of the living.
Wait for the LORD;
    be strong and take heart
    and wait for the LORD.

PSALM 27:13–14 NIV

The First Meeting

See to it that no one misses the grace of God and that no bitter root grows up to cause trouble and defile many.

HEBREWS 12:15 NIV

I remember the first time I met Eleanor, during Thanksgiving of 1993. I had been dating Barry, her son, for about six months, and he invited me to spend the holiday with his parents in Charleston, South Carolina. I was a student at Fuller Theological Seminary in Pasadena, California, and Barry worked for a television network in Orange County, so it was a flight from coast to coast for both of us.

As our plane left Atlanta, Georgia, on the final leg of our trip, I said, "Tell me about your mom."

He smiled. "Now, where would I start?"

"Are you two close?" I asked, trying to narrow the field.

"Yes, we're close," he replied. "Mom and Dad waited twelve years before they were able to have a child—and I'm it!"

Oh great! I thought. *I get to be "the other woman."*

I had talked with Eleanor a couple of times on the phone. Her strong Charleston accent was a match for my Scottish brogue any day. It reminded me of the gentle Southern accents in the movie *The Prince of Tides*. She always sounded warm and kind. "You sure are an answer to prayer," she once said. "We never knew what Barry was going to bring home!"

I had visions of stray dogs, Amazon women, biker chicks. Eleanor had watched me on television when I cohosted *The 700 Club*, so I was past first base. In her book I was definitely kosher.

"Mom talks a lot," Barry continued.

"My kind of woman!" I said.

"Yes . . . well, be prepared for Twenty Questions. Mom likes to know stuff."

"I have stuff," I answered. "Every woman has stuff."

When the plane began its descent into Charleston, I looked out the window at fields of swaying sweet grass and a multitude of little rivers running into each other, like veins connected to a throbbing human heart.

Later, as we began to walk up the jetway, I said to Barry, "You go first." I could see William and Eleanor standing at the end, looking anxiously through the crowd for their boy. William was about five-feet-eight with silver hair and a face creased from years of cracking jokes and worrying that the Depression might hit again. Eleanor was five-feet-two with beautiful red hair that complemented her lime green pantsuit. She held a single yellow rose in her hand.

Barry went to his mom first and hugged her, then to his dad. I stood back for a moment, allowing them some space, but Barry turned around and brought me forward. "Mom . . . Dad, this is Sheila."

Eleanor gave me the rose and reached out to hug me. "I feel like I know you," she said.

William smiled warmly and hugged me too. "I'm going to be on my best behavior while you're here," he said with a wink.

"Yeah, right, Dad." Barry laughed.

Barry led the way to the baggage claim with Eleanor beside him, and William and I brought up the rear. We all "small talked" for a while till our bags arrived, then we piled into an old, pale yellow Cadillac.

"Got it tuned to your station," William said to Barry as John Cougar Mellencamp's melody "Jack and Diane" filled the air. I admired the scenery as we crossed over the James Island Bridge onto James Island where they lived. Soon we turned into their street, Martello Drive, a charming road with pretty houses and manicured lawns and rocking chairs on front porches. William turned into number 353.

I immediately noticed the beautiful flowerbeds filled with multicolored pansies.

"Who has the green fingers?" I asked.

"That's Daddy," Eleanor replied. "He was featured once on the local news with his summer flowers."

"I'm a celebrity!" William added. "I'll show you the video if you like."

"I'd love that," I said with a smile.

As Barry and his dad took the luggage out of the car, Eleanor and I went in through the back door. The breakfast room and kitchen were paneled in a coffee-colored wood, and every available space was filled with knickknacks and souvenirs of past trips. One whole wall was covered with Barry's awards from grade school, high school, and college.

"I made Barry's favorite meal," Eleanor shouted from the kitchen as I sat down at the breakfast room table. "I hope you like it."

"I'm sure I will," I replied, hoping his favorite meal wasn't snails—but determined to eat them if it were.

Soon Barry came into the breakfast room, and William went into the kitchen to help Eleanor.

"Barry says you are a great cook!" I called out to Eleanor.

Barry looked at me with a puzzled expression. "When did I say that?"

I kicked him on the leg.

"Is there anything I can do to help?" I asked, poking my head around the kitchen door.

"It's all ready," William answered. He motioned for us to join him in the dining room. "Pull up at the table."

Eleanor joined us, carrying a covered casserole. William had already placed several other dishes on the table.

"Will you say grace, Sheila?" she asked me.

"You're the professional!" William added.

I rustled up my best professional grace, and we began to eat. The meal was enough to feed a small army: fried chicken, green beans with bacon and new potatoes, macaroni pie, squash, mashed potatoes and gravy, and corn bread.

If we eat like this for a week, I thought, *I'll end up looking like an entire group of people. We'll be able to show home movies on my butt!*

The food was delicious. Barry ate like a man who had been lost in a cave for two weeks.

"You're looking skinny," Eleanor said to Barry at the same time she cast a mildly accusing gaze at me. I thought of the low-fat dinners I cooked for him when he came to my apartment for dinner. "Perhaps you could give me some of your recipes," I said, scrambling for brownie points.

"You hate food like this," Barry said.

I kicked him again.

After dinner William and I volunteered to wash the dishes, and Eleanor and Barry sat in the living room catching up. When we were finished, we joined them.

"Oh my goodness!" I said as I looked around. I had just walked into the Shrine of Barry. On every wall, on every shelf, on every piece of furniture were photos of Barry from three months old to last Tuesday! Not just photos—also oil paintings and charcoal sketches.

I wonder if they have anything in velvet? I thought.

"I love this one," Eleanor said, pointing to a large oil that took up most of one wall. Barry must have been about fourteen; he was wearing a green leisure suit.

"Cool suit, Barry," I said, grinning.

"Right!" he replied.

We talked for a while and then decided to turn in for the night.

"You'll be in this room," Eleanor said as she walked me to the downstairs guest room, a pretty room decorated in pink and white. There was a large display case full of Madame Alexander dolls. All the Little Women from the book of the same name: Jo, Beth, Amy, Meg, and Marmie. Scarlett O'Hara in the green dress she fashioned from drapes before going to visit Rhett Butler to get money to save Tara—and another doll in her outrageous red hussy dress. Dorothy and Glenda, the Good Witch of the North, from *The Wizard of Oz*. Nancy Reagan. The dolls were all so per-fectly groomed and dressed, it seemed impossible that a child had ever played with them. Soon I knew why.

"I started collecting dolls when I turned forty," Eleanor said. "It's my hobby."

"How many do you have?"

"About five hundred," she replied. "I never had a daughter to buy them for, so I bought them for myself."

"They're beautiful." I thought back to my tomboy childhood when all I collected were boxes full of bugs and jars of tadpoles.

"Thanks for the lovely meal and for the rose," I said.

"You're very welcome," Eleanor replied as she left the room. Then she popped her head back in. "Oh, by the way. One of the things I like about you is that you're not all over Barry. I like that."

Mental note: Do not be "all over Barry" — whatever that means.

Saving Grace

I wanted to be strong, the kind of girl You'd smile upon.
I wanted to be known and yet I always stood alone.
Holding back my fears and questions, scared to bring them to Your door.
Longing for Your love and kindness, but so afraid You wanted more.

I tried to win Your heart. I tried to do more than my part.
I wanted You to see that You could always count on me
'Til finally the image crumbled, left me dying at Your feet.
And in the dust of all my trying. I was at the mercy seat.

Saving grace,
You are my saving grace.
I'm falling down on my face,
Covered by saving grace.
Saving grace
You are my saving grace.
Jesus, You took my place,
And now I live by saving grace.

And when they ask me,
"Who are you to stand and look so strong?"
I'll smile, and tell them
It's You I'm standing on.[1]

—FROM THE BLUE WATERS ALBUM

*E*leanor and William

The Next Morning

Deck the halls with boughs of holly,
And fourteen Christmas trees,
And twenty-eight wreaths,
And a silver cat,
And more angels than we are promised
for the Second Coming of Christ.

But by the grace of God I am what I am.

1 CORINTHIANS 15:10 NIV

I woke up about 7:00 A.M. I lay there for a while, wondering whether Barry was up and if the bathroom was free. Eventually I pulled a robe over my pajamas and went to the kitchen to see who else was up. William and Eleanor were sitting at the wooden table.

"Morning, princess," William said. "What would you like for breakfast?"

"Morning . . . Just coffee would be great."

"Coffee?" William said. "What kind of breakfast is that!"

Plenty, if you're still digesting four pounds of fried chicken, I thought.

Soon William reappeared with a bowl of fresh peaches, bacon, and toast.

"Barry told us you were in a mental hospital," Eleanor said.

I choked on my peaches, paused to collect myself, and then answered. "Yes, that's right. I was hospitalized for clinical depression in 1992." I looked directly at Eleanor as I assured her, "I'm much better now, honest!" I could feel peach juice dripping off my chin.

"Is Barry up yet?" I asked, making a mental note to kick him again.

"He won't be up till lunchtime," William answered. "Have you met my other baby?" He picked up a silver cat that had wandered into the kitchen. "This is Cinder." He gazed at the cat with the adoring eyes of a proud mother.

"She's beautiful . . . How old is she?"

"Twenty-one years old! . . . She used to crawl in bed with Barry and keep his feet warm."

"I never knew that," I said with a smile.

"I'm sure there are a few things you don't know," Eleanor added.

"Oh . . . you're probably right," I said, wondering what on earth she meant and pretty sure she would tell me at some point. "I guess that goes both ways," I replied and then could have kicked myself. I was already an official loony. What else did they need?

Then Eleanor announced the agenda for the day. "When Barry gets up, we'll finish the Christmas decorations."

There's more? I thought, patting myself on the back that it didn't come out of my overzealous mouth. I had never seen so many decorations in my life.

Three papier-mâché choirboys stood by the fireplace. They

were so enormous, they looked as if they were on steroids. And in every window she had a wreath with a big red velvet bow, probably twenty in all, maybe twenty-eight. And throughout the house were enough thick garlands to string over the Grand Canyon. And on every table, and hanging from different corners of the ceiling, were spray-painted angels (not quite as many as when Christ returns, but almost).

I was not used to such profuse decorating, since my own mother is not big on this; it brings back too many painful memories of a Christmas she would rather forget. In December of 1959 my father was in intensive care, and every night as she dragged herself home, the Christmas lights on the tree and the paper chains seemed to mock the unraveling of her life.

Eventually Barry surfaced. "How long have you been up?" he asked.

"Oh, about four days."

Once he'd had breakfast, we all went Christmas shopping. It's a blur to me now. William, a seasoned veteran at this, stayed in the car. I, the naive novice, attempted to keep up with Barry and Eleanor. There's no need to list everything they purchased. Let me just say this. I took two Tylenol P.M. that night, but still had nightmares that I was being chased by hordes of gold, spray-painted angels trying to tie me up in tinsel.

I have only recently gotten rid of the twitch.

That Conversation

> I cry aloud to the LORD;
> I lift up my voice to the LORD for mercy.
>
> PSALM 142:1 NIV

It was our last morning in Charleston. My bags were packed and waiting at the door. Barry was still sleeping. Big surprise! Eleanor and William and I sat around the breakfast table. William was reading his paper. Eleanor and I were enjoying a cup of coffee.

"There's just something I have to tell you, Sheila," she said.

Well, this is it! I thought. My mind raced. What secret could she reveal? Barry was born a girl and had a sex-change operation? He was adopted at birth and is the rightful heir to the British throne? He has only two weeks to live?

"Barry has not always lived a good Christian life," she began. "When he was in college, he did some things he shouldn't have done . . . I know he drank beer! And he seemed a little too friendly with one of the girls—if you know what I mean."

She hung all over him, I thought.

The whole fairly innocent diatribe lasted for more than an hour. Yet she told me nothing I didn't already know from Barry.

"How do you know all this?" I asked. "Did Barry tell you?"

"No . . . When he was home I'd listen in on his phone calls."

I nearly choked on my coffee. I slid down in my chair. I had said nothing in an hour. William had said nothing in an hour. I turned to him. "Anything to add, Pop?"

"Yeah! Look at Cinder!"

Surprised by his reply, I looked at the cat. She was sitting in a chair, looking out of the window. That's all. No juggling, no playing the piano, just sitting there being a cat.

"That's typical of you, William," Eleanor said as she picked up the coffee cups and headed into the kitchen, obviously disappointed in both of us. In me, because I wasn't horrified at Barry's college days. In William, because when things got tense in the house, he looked at the cat. It was a pattern I was to become familiar with.

Later, as Barry and I were on the flight home to California, I thought about Eleanor's words. "I think your mom tried to scare me off," I said to Barry.

"Really!" he replied. "So . . . is this it?"

"Not a chance!"

Mental note: Send William a present for the cat.

The Search for the Ring

A token of our endless love,
A gift of sacrifice,
A stab to someone else's heart,
A stealing of her prize.

*I*n April 1994 Barry went back to visit his parents. I was
unaware of this momentous event until Barry told me about
it after our engagement. While there, Barry told his parents he
wanted to look for engagement rings.

"I want to come with you, Barry," Eleanor said.

"I kind of wanted to do this by myself, Mom."

"It's a lot of money, honey . . . I'm coming."

Begrudgingly, Barry agreed, and they soon were walking into a
prominent Charleston jewelry shop.

"I'd like to look at engagement rings, please," Barry said to the
jeweler who welcomed them into his shop and soon began pulling
tray after tray of diamonds out of the glass display case.

Barry looked carefully at each tray, removing a couple of rings
and holding them up to the light. Finally he said, "I like this one.
How much is it?"

The jeweler gave him the price.

"That's ridiculous!" Eleanor said.

"It's a lovely stone, ma'am," the jeweler replied.

Eleanor turned to look directly at her son. "Well, you'll need something in writing from her then."

"What do you mean, Mom?"

"You'll need a written promise that if she doesn't go through with the wedding, you get the ring back."

Barry felt as if his mom had humiliated him in front of the jeweler, so he left the store immediately—with Eleanor following dutifully behind. Once they were back home, he told her how inappropriate her statement had been.

"I was just trying to protect you," she said. "I don't feel you can trust anybody anymore."

After that discussion I imagine Eleanor sitting there for a long time, her mind turning over and over. *Will she love him enough? Will she ever hurt him? Will she shut me out?*

It was a cold night in Charleston.

The Ring

I always thank God for you because of his grace given you in Christ Jesus.

1 CORINTHIANS 1:4 NIV

As Barry and I drove along Pacific Coast Highway toward our favorite Italian restaurant in Laguna Beach, I thought Barry was ill. His palms were sweating. He was pale and distracted. I had no idea he was about to propose.

"If you'd rather not go out for dinner tonight, that's fine with me, babe," I said.

"No! No, I'm fine . . . really. Really, I'm fine."

"Well, you don't look fine," I answered. "I wonder if you're getting the flu?"

Laguna Beach is a tourist's paradise, so the narrow streets are always filled with cars; so are the few parking lots. Finally we found a parking spot and walked over to the restaurant, where a lot of people were sitting in the entranceway, waiting for tables.

"Do you think we should try somewhere else?" I asked.

Just then a waiter pushed through the crowd to greet us and led us to a great table. I still didn't have a clue. Barry looked worse. The waiter gave us menus. I looked at mine. Something was wrong with it. I couldn't find chicken anywhere. Then I read it.

"I love you with all my heart. Will you marry me?"

Suddenly I realized that everyone in the restaurant was looking at us.

"Yes!" I said, stunned, surreal.

Then out of the kitchen came a camera crew with lots of lights, followed by some of our best friends. It was so bizarre! Barry produced the most beautiful ring I had ever seen, and it fit. I almost threw up. I'm so glad I didn't! The whole evening was a whirlwind of joy and laughter and hope and tears.

And Barry finally looked normal.

The next morning I called my mother in Scotland. She was very excited for me. Then we called Barry's mom and dad. They were happy. I took the phone into another room so I could talk privately with his mom. "Eleanor, I will never take your place. You are Barry's mom forever. I want us to be friends, but it will take two of us."

"I want that too," she said.

I knew she meant it. I also knew it would be hard.

Planning the Wedding

To you, O LORD, I called; to the Lord I cried for mercy.

PSALM 30:8 NIV

(Oh boy, did I cry for mercy!!)

One day in August of 1994 the Pfaehlers and the Walshes met in my apartment in Laguna Niguel, California. My mom, Betty Walsh, was staying with me, and William and Eleanor were staying with Barry. We were planning the wedding.

"Something small. That's all I ask. Something small," I said.

Most of my audience did not agree with me. My mom did, but that's to be expected. Eleanor and Barry did not. William was wondering how the cat would look in a tuxedo!

"I just don't want a big expensive fuss with a bunch of people we hardly know," I said.

Barry leaned forward in his chair, then he spoke. "I've waited all my life for this. And I only intend to do this once. I want it to be perfect."

"I've only got one child," Eleanor added. "Are you going to deny me the wedding I've dreamed of since Barry was born?"

I retreated to the bathroom in tears. I thought it would help! It didn't. We met again the next day. Same apartment. Same people, with the same opinions.

"Okay!" I said. "Here's the deal. I don't want a big wedding." I looked at Barry. "You do. And you have that right. So go ahead, but you need to understand that I'm not going to run around like a chicken with its head cut off. If you want this, you have to do it. I'm not going to help. I'll show up with joy written in every line of my face—but that's it."

"That's great!" Barry said.

"Absolutely!" Eleanor agreed.

Unfortunately, she thought I would change my mind as the day got closer. I didn't.

William, Eleanor, Mum, my dog Bentley, and me

The Week of the Wedding

Chestnuts roasting on an open fire,
Vessels bursting on your nose.
Tempers are frayed like the edge of a quilt,
And blood is boiling to your toes.

But you, O LORD, have mercy on me; raise me up, that I
may repay them.

PSALM 41:10 NIV

Two nights before the wedding, Barry and his mom sat
around two long banquet tables covered with greenery and
flowers and ribbon, positioned in Emily Schroeder's driveway.
(Emily was a friend known for her green thumb.) Eleanor had
pins in her mouth and was twisting ribbons into huge bows for the
table arrangements for the rehearsal dinner and the reception.

"I can't believe she's off entertaining her family while I'm here
arranging all these flowers," Eleanor fumed out of the side of her
mouth, trying not to swallow the pins.

"Well, she told you, Mom, that she wouldn't get involved in a
big wedding," Barry said, trying to return his mother's blood pressure to something close to acceptable.

"I didn't think she meant it quite like this. This is ridiculous!"

"Come on, Mom. This is what we wanted!"

"I just hoped she would want it too."

Eleanor sat down and cried. She was trying so hard, and it seemed as if no one had noticed.

The Rehearsal Dinner

For what we are about to receive,
May God have mercy on us all.

I had never been to a rehearsal dinner before. It's an American tradition. In Scotland you just show up for the wedding—and hope for the best. It usually works. Although one time it didn't.

My sister, Frances, was being married in our home church, Ayr Baptist. She was a beautiful bride and it was a lovely ceremony. At the end of the service, one of our former church members, who had since moved, decided to slip out quickly and get some photos of the bride and groom as they descended the front stairs. He opened a door at the front of the church, which used to be a way out of the sanctuary when he was a member, and closed it quietly behind him. But now this door opened into a broom cupboard.

The rest of us knew that. Everyone saw him go in. Some watched in horror. Others (with the gift of mercy!) were laughing so hard, they could have burst a blood vessel. Eventually he came out and appeared at the reception looking very dusty.

Rehearsal dinners seem to bring out the worst in people. I

guess the reason is nerves. On December 2, 1994, we all gathered at St. Matthew's Lutheran Church for the run-through of the service. The bridesmaids were there, the groomsmen, Barry's family, my family, and the two pastors who would be taking part. My sister, Frances, was there to rehearse the song she would be singing. The whole thing dragged on too long for her two sons, who started playing tag around the altar.

Barry lost it. "You can't run around in here," he yelled. "This is the house of God!"

I was so mad, I yelled back. "What did Jesus say about 'suffer little children to come unto me'?"

"That's about the most stupid thing I've heard you say!" he returned.

"Don't call me stupid in front of my family!"

"Well, perhaps they could leave!"

And they did, very shortly after that. Everyone slipped out of the church and headed for the Charleston Country Club for the dinner. Barry and I got into his car and drove in silence. When we got there, he refused to go in.

"You've got to go in," I said. "Everyone is waiting for us. Your parents paid for this . . . Your mother will kill you!"

We sat there in silence for a few more moments.

Then Barry turned toward me and put his arm around my shoulder. "You know what?" he said. "I don't really care what anyone else wants or thinks. I just want us to be happy."

We kissed. And, of course, we went in.

The meal was lovely. Then came the speeches. Big mistake!

William made a short, touching little speech. Then it was my brother's turn to reply on behalf of my family. He was halfway to his feet when Eleanor stood up.

"Well!" she said. "I wouldn't call what William delivered a speech. There's a lot more to say."

Barry and I began to sink lower in our chairs.

Eleanor's speech lasted forty-five minutes! She told everyone everything. She talked about our breakups, about how she never thought we'd make it. Then she told how sad she'd felt when she'd had a heart attack a few years earlier. "I never thought I would live to see Barry married," she said.

She went on to tell them about the time Barry and I called her from Scotland; when the operator asked if she would accept a call from the United Kingdom, she thought he said the Magic Kingdom and wanted to know why we were at Disneyland! People started to laugh. Eleanor took this as a desire for an encore. Her speech went on and on. Some people were bent double, they were laughing so hard. She had the time of her life! And she did not forget to tell them how long it took to do the floral arrangements for the tables. She was the hit of the evening.

After the dinner we went back to the Pfaehlers's house for coffee.

"Are you going to help with the flower arrangements in the morning?" Eleanor asked me.

"No, Mom," I said. "I have hair and makeup appointments."

"Well, who's going to decorate the twelve-foot Christmas tree and the fourteen little trees!!" she said rather pitifully.

I was speechless. I thought, *Where can I hide till it's all over?*

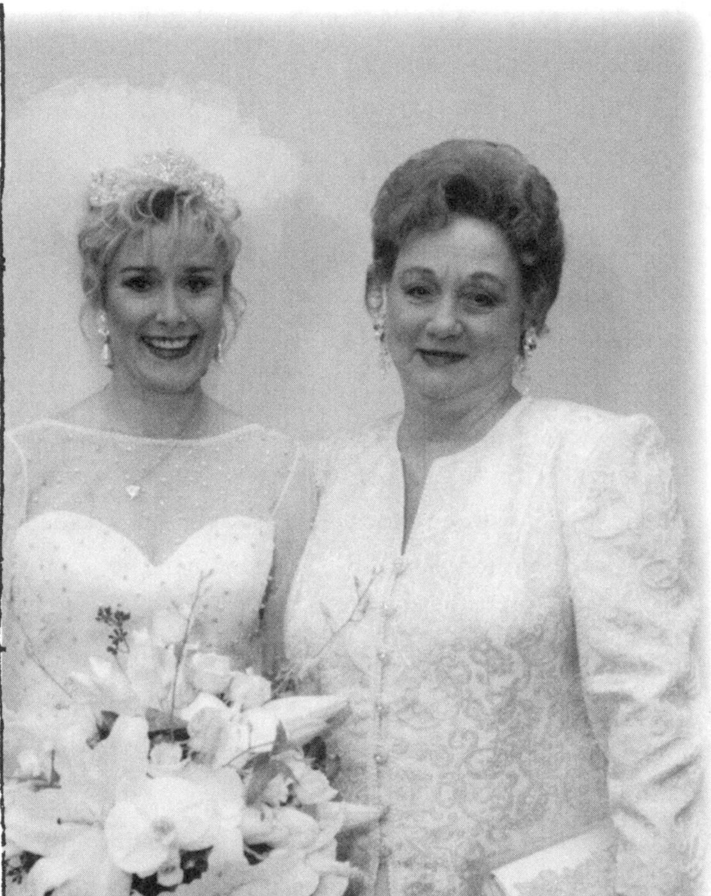

The Big Day: December 3, 1994

A fine romance, do we dare to take a chance?
The Father set His heart upon a fine romance.

Grace and peace to you from God our Father and the Lord
Jesus Christ.

EPHESIANS 1:2 NIV

Saturday, December 3, was a beautiful day. I woke up to sun-shine streaming through the windows of my room at Charleston's Meeting Street Inn. That night this same luxurious bedroom would be our honeymoon suite.

I looked at my dress, hanging on the outside of the wardrobe. It was so beautiful! I knew I would feel like a fairy princess in it. I was so happy! I had a shower and put on jeans and a sweater and went for a walk. The wedding ceremony was at four in the after-noon, so I had time to wander.

At noon I met my mom and Frances at the beauty salon. We all got wedding hairdos and had our makeup done. My mom never wears much makeup—a little foundation, powder, and a touch of blush. She doesn't wear lipstick or eye makeup. I told the girl to give her the works. She looked beautiful.

The limousine arrived for me at 3:30. I had my gown in a

garment bag so I could change at the church. When the car pulled up outside St. Matthew's Lutheran Church, I struggled out of the door with my bags and gown. Then I saw Eleanor. She looked at me with a strange, dazed expression. Realizing how difficult it was for me to carry a poofy, Cinderella wedding gown with everything else, she started to come toward me. Then she said, "Oh no, I can't. I'm just like a zombie," and went inside.

I had no idea what she was talking about. The limo driver helped me inside, and then I asked him to go check on my mother-in-law-to-be.

The bridesmaids and I had so much fun getting ready. My matron of honor, Nancy Goudie, had been my best friend since I was sixteen. She had flown over from the United Kingdom for the wedding. I had four bridesmaids and two darling blond-haired, twin flower girls. We all laughed and talked as we fixed each other's hair. Then Eleanor fell through the door of the dressing room like the survivor of a train wreck.

"Mom, what's wrong?" I asked, as she sank into a chair.

"It's all a mess," she said. "It's all going wrong! It's a disaster!"

"What's going wrong?" I asked Eleanor as I fetched a glass of water for her.

"Your father-in-law has no bow tie!"

I tried not to laugh. She had worked so hard, so very hard to make this the perfect day she had always imagined, and the rental place had forgotten Pop's bow tie, which apparently was a bad omen to her.

"Mom, that's all right. Someone can lend him one. Don't

worry. It'll be okay. There are no bad omens, just bad hairdos . . . God's here. We'll be fine."

We all tried to settle her down.

Then it was time. My thoughts turned to my dad. He died when I was four years old, but at moments like these I missed him as acutely as if he had died the week before. Yet my brother, Stephen, was standing at the back of the church with me, and he was now the age my dad was when he died. It seemed like a gift to have him there. That's how Stephen has always seemed to me, a gift.

Sounds of my homeland filled the air. A lone bagpipe player piped the mothers down the aisle, playing my mother's favorite Scottish melody. Then it was my turn. As I walked toward Barry on the arm of my brother, I could have skipped. I could have run. I was so happy!

During the ceremony Barry and I took communion. He seemed restless at my side, wishing it were over. Finally we walked down the aisle together as Mr. and Mrs. Barry Pfaehler and were off to the reception at the Charleston Society Hall. A blur! A beginning. A wonderful beginning. That's all I could think of.

The band we had hired was double booked, so they had sent a backup. They were so bad, it was hilarious. The trumpet player had the worst toupee I'd ever seen; it looked as if he'd killed a cat on the way to the reception and superglued it to his head. His glasses were held on with a huge rubber band.

I said to the photographer, "I don't care how many photos you get of Barry and me, just make sure you get plenty of the trumpet player!"

Barry and I were so busy talking to people, we didn't have time to eat, so the caterer said he would make a basket for us to take to the hotel. As we got ready to leave, we asked him for it. He sheepishly told us that someone had set fire to our basket and our supper had burned! And all the rest of the food was gone. (I love this stuff!!)

One more hitch. The limo driver had gotten drunk and left. Barry and I stood in our "going away" outfits, waving good-bye to everyone at the reception and wondering what to do next. Then William rose to the occasion. "I'll drive you!"

We all laughed the whole way to our honeymoon suite. (God has such a cool sense of humor.)

The next morning I asked Barry about the limousine. "Didn't it seem a little strange to you? I mean, the driver looked at me like he was giving me his condolences."

Barry laughed. "My dad got a bargain."

"What do you mean, he got a bargain?"

"He got the limo from his friend at Stuhr's Funeral Home!"

We laughed till we cried.

Sonnet

Let me not to the marriage of true minds
Admit impediments: love is not love
Which alters when it alteration finds,
Or bends with the remover to remove.
Oh no! it is an ever-fixèd mark,
That looks on tempests and is never shaken;
It is the star to every wandering bark,
Whose worth's unknown, although his height be taken.
Love's not Time's fool, though rosy lips and cheeks
Within his bending sickle's compass come;
Love alters not with brief hours and weeks,
But bears it out even to the edge of doom.
    If this be error and upon me proved,
    I never writ, nor no man ever loved.[2]

—WILLIAM SHAKESPEARE

The First Year

For this reason a man will leave* his father and mother and
be united to his wife, and they will become one flesh.

GENESIS 2:24 NIV

(*Always assuming they've read that part!)

We made our home in Nashville, Tennessee, close to some of our best friends. And Barry kept in regular contact with his mom and dad by telephone.

"What do you mean, every day?" I said, the week after the wedding. "Who talks to their parents every day?!"

"Honey! Chill a little here," Barry said. "That's just been our pattern. But we can choose now. You find your own comfort level here. It's okay . . . Don't lay an egg!"

I must admit I overreact. I try to pass it off as a spiritual gift, but it's getting harder and harder to do that.

Then, only a few weeks later, Eleanor and William drove ten hours from Charleston to share our first Christmas with us. I was not happy. I wanted to be alone, just the two of us. After all, Barry and I had only been married for three weeks. Then I thought of all Eleanor did to make the wedding so lovely. I tried to ask myself, "What is Christmas? Surely it's a time to gather with those you love and celebrate Christ, the Gift."

So I ate a whole fruitcake and decided to have fun.

When the Pfaehlers arrived, William began to unpack the car. As whole hams, crates of tinned vegetables, pounds and pounds of oranges, and enough toilet tissue to see us through a national outbreak of dysentery came into the house, I asked Barry, "What does your dad know that we don't?"

"That's just my dad," Barry said, sighing. "He can't pass up a bargain. He thinks the Depression could hit again at any moment."

"Well, we're covered!"

On Christmas Eve I discovered a new side of Eleanor. She is fun! And a good sport. We decided to go to Opryland for the annual Christmas in the Park celebration. It was so cold. Eleanor wore her fur coat, and the rest of us bundled up in sheepskin jackets and hats and scarves. There were carolers dressed in Victorian costumes, hot apple cider, Christmas lights (almost as many as at William and Eleanor's house). But after an hour we were so cold we could hardly talk. Then I saw the carousel.

"Barry, look!" I cried. "The carousel is working. Let's ride it!"

"Have you lost your marbles?" he said. "You'd freeze to death."

"Oh please," I whined like a four-year-old. I was getting nowhere.

"Come on. Let's do it!" Eleanor said.

I looked at her in amazement. "Help me up," she said.

That's one of my most vivid memories of Eleanor. There she was sitting on a carousel, holding a cat inside her fur coat to keep it warm, the cat's tail sticking out behind her as if it were her own.

Afterward we went home and sat by the fire and sang carols.

Mental note: Eleanor is a good sport.

The Baby!

For you created my inmost being;
*   you knit me together in my mother's womb.*
I praise you because I am fearfully and wonderfully made;
*   your works are wonderful,*
*   I know that full well.*
My frame was not hidden from you
*   when I was made in the secret place.*
When I was woven together in the depths of the earth,
*   your eyes saw my unformed body.*
All the days ordained for me
*   were written in your book*
*   before one of them came to be.*

PSALM 139:13–16 NIV

*I*n early March 1996 I was cleaning out the bathroom cupboards in our home in Laguna Niguel. I had bought a six-pack of pregnancy tests at Sam's Club because Barry and I had been trying to have a child, and I had one test kit left. We had just received word from our doctors that our chances of conceiving were almost impossible. I almost threw the last test kit out, and then I thought, *Why don't I just take it?*

I left it sitting on the window ledge and went to make myself a cup of tea. When I came back to continue cleaning, I saw the square box and picked it up to throw in the trash. Out of the corner of my eye, I saw what looked like a plus sign. I couldn't believe it was true; I thought, *It might be past the sell-by date.* So I went to the store and bought another test. This time I watched that box like a hawk—and there it was again, the little red cross.

I stared at it in disbelief. My first thought was, *When do I tell Barry? Do I call him at work and tell him? Do I wait till he comes home?* I knew he'd be over the moon. *What about presenting it to him at dinner, on top of his pork chop?*

Then I stopped and looked at myself in the mirror—I was grinning from ear to ear. *I'm going to be a mommy. I'm pregnant!* . . . *But I'm forty! Help!*

I found myself wondering if the hospital would be willing to give me an epidural in the eighth month. Then I thought, *I'll be fine. I've had things out before. Two teeth!*

I called Scotland to tell my sister about my thoughts. I couldn't tell if she could still hear me. She seemed to be lying on the floor laughing—and muttering something about my not having a clue.

I called my mom. She was over the moon. We called Eleanor and William. They were too.

"We have lots of good family names," Eleanor said.

Oh great! I thought. *I wonder if Christ might return before the baby's born?*

Then it was time for the first ultrasound.

"Do you want to know the sex of the baby?" the nurse asked.

"Yes!" Barry and I cried in unison.

"It's a boy!"

"A boy! A boy!!" we both shouted.

I was excited for two reasons. I was a tomboy, so a boy would be fun. We'd get to play soccer and climb trees and . . . I wouldn't have to inherit Eleanor's doll collection.

What a pathetic thought to pass through a human heart at a time like this. But it was one of the first things I thought. She had over five hundred dolls. I'm not a doll person. I would drown in that many dolls. But it was a boy! Hallelujah!

I couldn't believe it. I was forty and having my first baby!

Now came the big issue. Who would be with me in the delivery room? I didn't want anyone but Barry. (I had no idea that when the time came I would have accepted help from the Domino's Pizza delivery guy!)

Next big question. Who'll get to visit first? Barry left it up to me. I wanted my mom. I called Scotland to talk to her. She changed my mind. "This is Eleanor and William's only grandchild, Sheila. I already have three," she said. "This will probably be the only time they'll get to do this. Don't you think it would be a gift to let them be there first?"

I hung up the receiver and then called Eleanor to invite her to be the first one with us. She cried.

Mental note: Send my mom a big bunch of flowers.

The Delivery

You are fairer than the sons of men;
Grace is poured upon Your lips;
Therefore God has blessed You forever.

PSALM 45:2 NKJV

*I*n October 1996 I was at the doctor's office for my eighth-month checkup. I always thought it a strange irony that her office was near Fashion Island in Newport Beach, one of the best malls in America. After every appointment I would go to that mall, sit by the fountain, and watch skinny women pass by with bags full of clothes that wouldn't fit me any longer.

During that appointment the doctor asked me, "What day do you want to have the baby, Sheila?"

"What do you mean? I thought that was God's job."

"Not any more." She put her stethoscope down on her desk and laughed. "We choose the day. Now, here's the deal. I'm going on vacation on December 20. So how does the thirteenth sound?"

"Fine, I guess," I said, a little stunned. "How do you do that? Do I have to jump around a lot on the twelfth?"

"No, no!" she said. "I'll give you something."

(Note to reader: not a good idea. Stick with God's basic plan. It works better.)

Well, she gave me something all right, and I immediately went into hard labor. *So much for all the jolly birthing and breathing classes I went through*, I thought.

I was in labor for thirteen hours. It seemed like a week. I thought I was going to die. Then, at 5:20 in the morning of December 13, 1996, there he was! So tiny. Such a loud cry, just like his mom. I was speechless. He was perfect. What a miracle! My baby blue.

Lay your tiny golden head upon this pillow, dear.
There are angels watching over you.
And the Morning Star is in the heavens, Baby Blue.

Can you see the moon is shining in your room,
Tying silver ribbons in your hair?
May your sleep be sweet until the sun brings morning here.

And I never knew such a tender love
That could break my heart in two,
So I lie down gently now at Jesus' feet with you.

And I feel I'm lying on holy ground.
Such a gift from God, Baby Blue.
So I kiss your velvet cheek and say a prayer for you.

With love, Mommy

The only stretch mark I have left is in my soul.

The Visits

And He said to me, "My grace is sufficient for you, for My strength is made perfect in weakness."

2 CORINTHIANS 12:9 NKJV

It was the best of times . . .

Whenever Eleanor and William came to visit, they helped with all they had. Eleanor would fold the laundry. William loved to cook spaghetti or okra soup (whatever that is!). He is a hard-working man who finds it very hard to sit down and rest; our garage has never been as clean as after one of their visits.

But William's favorite thing to do was to rock Christian to sleep. One night I was upstairs working in my office, and William was in Christian's room. I always kept the baby monitor on in my office, as it's the only room in which I can't hear his cries. I suddenly became aware of the fact that William was singing to Christian. I bent over the monitor to listen. William could not remember the words to any of the traditional lullabies, so he made up his own!

> *You've got sugar dripping off your feet,*
> *Papa's boy, and you sure are sweet.*

Rummie tummie tum, and a rum tum tum.
You've got sugar dripping off your feet.

It was the same with Eleanor. She loved to sing, "patty cake, patty cake, baker's man," and Christian would clap along. But the one that nearly drove me up the wall was when she would sing:

Diddle diddle dumpling, my son John
Went to bed with his stockings on;
One shoe on and one shoe off,
Diddle diddle dumpling, my son John.

It took every ounce of strength I had to keep from saying, "It's, 'One shoe *off* and one shoe *on!*' Can't you hear it? It doesn't rhyme the other way. The kid's name isn't Joff."

Mental note: Try to find a book on being delivered from being so anal.

It was the worst of times . . .

But the fruit of the Spirit is love, joy, peace, patience, kindness, goodness, faithfulness, gentleness and self-control. Against such things there is no law.

GALATIANS 5:22–23 NIV

Barry and I had to go out of town overnight. William and Eleanor were staying at our house. I was grateful they had always made themselves at home; I find it easier to have guests who just fit in and help themselves to what they want . . . I just had no idea how at home they felt!

We got back the next day just after lunch, and I went into the pantry to get a tin of soup. It wasn't there. In fact there was nothing there that should have been there. I stared for a few moments, wondering if I needed glasses.

Then Eleanor came into the kitchen. "We moved everything around," she said. "This is better."

Better for whom? I wondered. "Where's the soup?" I asked, trying to rustle up the fruit of the Spirit.

"Over there," she said, pointing to the other side of the kitchen.

"But that's where the pots and pans are," I said, slow to catch on.

"Not anymore. They're in here," she answered, opening a different cupboard.

"Well, la di da!" I said and headed to the bathroom to mutter into the toilet. After a few moments and a quick chorus of "I Surrender All," I headed back and bumped into a table.

That wasn't there when we left, I thought. I looked around the room. Everything was moved. Pictures were hanging in different places; lamps stood on different tables.

I went to the mall and ate four pieces of pizza.

When I look back now, I think that Eleanor and I spent a lot of time muttering and not much time telling each other the truth. Of course, we had no idea what was just around the corner . . .

Part Two

The Turning

The LORD is my shepherd; I shall not want.
He makes me to lie down in green pastures;
He leads me beside the still waters.
He restores my soul;
He leads me in the paths of righteousness
For His name's sake.
Yea, though I walk through the valley of the
*   shadow of death,*
I will fear no evil;
For You are with me;
Your rod and Your staff, they comfort me.

PSALM 23:1–4 NKJV

The Beginning

Therefore we do not lose heart. Though outwardly we are wasting away, yet inwardly we are being renewed day by day.

2 CORINTHIANS 4:16 NIV

*I*n spring of 1997 Barry called his parents for their weekly chat. As he talked, I could see his shoulders sag and his eyes begin to narrow. Then he passed the phone to me with a troubled look on his face.

I didn't know what to expect, so I began with my usual greeting. "Hi, Mom. How are you doing?"

"Not so good, Sheila. Not so good," she answered. "I didn't feel well last night, and Pop took me to the emergency room in case it was my heart."

"What did they find, Mom?" I asked, concern rising.

For a moment the line was silent. Then Eleanor said, "Well, it's not my heart, but they found some polyps on my colon."

"What does that mean?" I asked. "Could they tell if they were malignant or benign?"

"No, I have to have more tests, and they'll see if they're cancerous."

Not long after that Eleanor called to tell us the results of the tests. The polyps were cancerous. In May of that same year the doctors operated and thought they had removed them all.

We prayed and waited for the eventual checkups we hoped would confirm Eleanor's complete recovery . . .

Lamb of God, sweet rose of heaven,
Gift of grace and Lord of life,
Holy One for sinners given,
Come, fill Your child tonight.

We wait now in Your presence.
We kneel before Your throne.
For You alone are worthy,
O Lion of Judah,
Sweet rose of heaven.

Lamb of God, sweet rose of heaven,
Gift of grace and Lord of life,
Holy One for sinners given,
Come, fill Your child tonight.

We wait now in Your presence.
We kneel before Your throne.
For You alone are worthy,
O Lion of Judah,
Sweet rose of heaven.

In November Eleanor went back for a six-month checkup. The cancer had spread to her liver. That was a very dark week.

There is nothing much they can do for liver cancer. It's a ravenous beast. Eleanor had sixty doses of chemotherapy. Her body handled it fairly well: She lost a little hair, but not much. Her red hair was still gorgeous, without even a touch of gray. She was nauseous and had bad diarrhea. She got very tired.

Eleanor adjusted to the discomfort with remarkable courage. It's one of the things I found so paradoxical about her. If Barry had his hair cut really short, she had a fit. If my hair was too long or my dress was the wrong color, she would tell me. Yet when she was faced with a terminal illness, she was calm and strong.

Mental note: Write a book and call it
Don't Sweat the Big Stuff.

The Gift

Three times I pleaded with the Lord to take it away from me. But he said to me, "My grace is sufficient for you, for my power is made perfect in weakness." Therefore I will boast all the more gladly about my weaknesses, so that Christ's power may rest on me.

2 CORINTHIANS 12:8–9 NIV

*I*t was the worst time to be given the best invitation. Christian was only a few weeks old; Mom had just received her cancer diagnosis; and Pop had had a knee replacement surgery that left him in more pain than before the operation. It was then that I was invited to join the five other speakers on the Women of Faith team.

I knew Barbara Johnson. I had heard of Luci Swindoll and Patsy Clairmont, but Marilyn Meberg and Thelma Wells were new names and faces to me. I had heard great things about what this team was doing. It seemed right up my alley. They are all a little out in left field, a couple of sandwiches short of a picnic, if you know what I mean! I would fit right in.

I knew this conference was beginning to pack out arenas across the country, so I talked to Eleanor and William about this opportunity. My big concern was that we would be on the road too much; I wanted to be with them as much as possible. They both encouraged me to accept this wonderful invitation.

The first conference was in Hawaii and went by without a hitch. Then we hit number two and a major roadblock. I had asked the host church to provide a baby-sitter for Christian while I was on stage. No problem, they said. That evening I was in my dressing room, changing Christian's diaper, when "The Baby-Sitter" came in. She was about twelve or thirteen years old with nails the size of small snakes. Painted purple!

She'll poke his eye out! I thought, wondering, as a sidebar, *Just when, exactly, did I become like my mother?*

*M*y buddies, the Women of Faith

I'm sure the baby-sitter was a lovely girl, and I love purple nail polish—but as a new mom, I panicked. I paid her and found her a seat at the conference. That whole weekend the six Women of Faith just passed Christian back and forth to whoever was not speaking at the time. It was awful!

When we got home, I called Eleanor to see how she was and told her what had happened. Later that evening she called back. "William and I have been talking, and we've come to a decision."

"About what, Mom?" I asked.

"About your problem on the road. William and I are going to travel with you."

I couldn't believe I had heard her right. Who would make such a sacrifice? "You can't do that," I said. "What about your chemotherapy and Pop's bad knee?"

"I'll take your speaking schedule to the doctor tomorrow. He'll have to fit the chemo around it."

And that's what she did. What a gift. What a gift of grace!

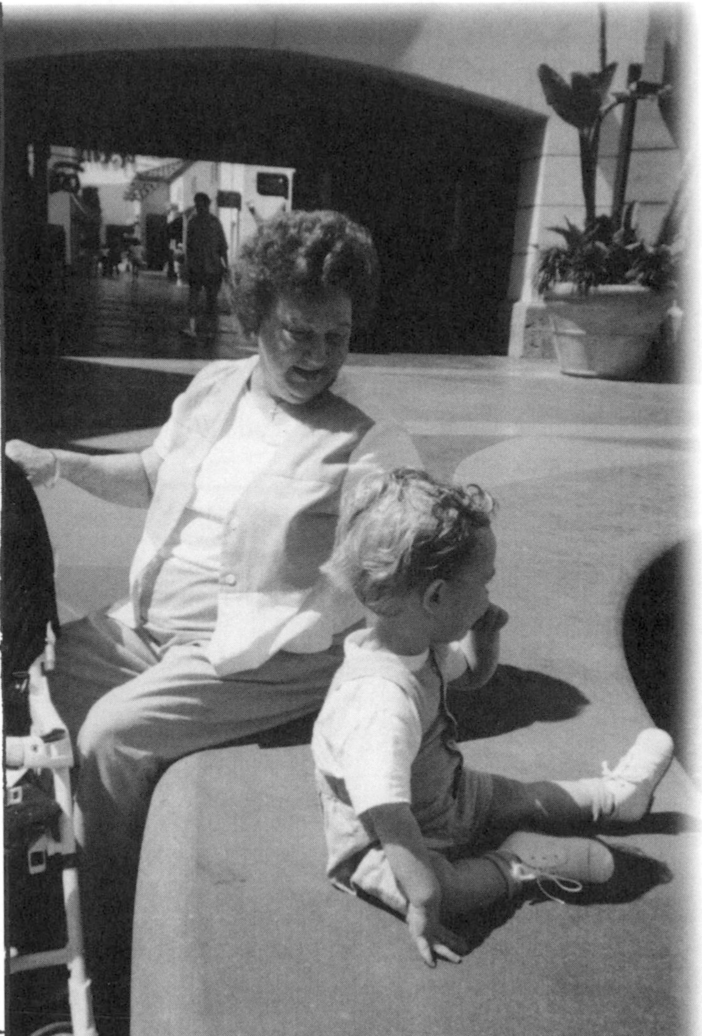

A Second Opinion

For Your mercy is great above the heavens,
And Your truth reaches to the clouds.

PSALM 108:4 NKJV

*I*n January of 1998 I called Eleanor to see how she was feeling. We chatted a while, and then she said, "I'm not sure my doctors are telling me everything. I just want to know what the whole truth is. I'd like to know how long I have."

I heard the pain in her voice and wanted to do everything I could to help. "Why don't you come to Nashville? One of the best cancer specialists in the country is at Baptist Hospital," I said. "I'll go with you, and we will get a second opinion."

The next month Eleanor and William came for a visit with all her medical records. William, or Bubsie as we fondly refer to him, didn't want to go to the doctor's office, so Barry and I drove down to Baptist Hospital with Eleanor.

Soon we were all seated in the doctor's office, waiting for him to give Eleanor a countdown of her days.

The doctor was kind and straight. "Let me make one thing clear," he said. "I'm a doctor, but I'm also a Christian. I know that what I tell you is from the best of my experience, but I also know that your days are in God's hands and they are marked down in His book."

The doctor went through all of the charts and then said,

"Okay. The bottom line is, you have six months to two years. You have had sixty chemotherapy shots, and there is a new kind of treatment we can give you as a final last lap. You need to wait until there are some physical signs. Your skin will turn yellow, you will get pain in your left shoulder, and your liver will enlarge."

Mom asked, "What will this regimen do for me?"

"All it will do is buy you a little more time."

"How sick will I be?"

The doctor admitted that she would be pretty sick.

Eleanor thought for only a moment. Then she replied, "I will opt not to do that."

"I respect that," he answered, but we could see a quizzical look in his eyes, so she explained.

"The reason is, I have a grandson." Then she started to cry. "I want to be able to enjoy him and spend time with him every day I have left."

We thanked the doctor for being so straightforward and left. We drove in silence for a while and then pulled into one of our favorite little spots for coffee.

I took Eleanor's hand. "Are you afraid, Mom?"

"No, I'm not afraid . . . I don't want to die—but I'm not afraid." Then her tears began to flow. "I don't want Christian to forget me."

We all sat in silence with tears running down our faces.

> But You, O GOD the Lord,
> Deal with me for Your name's sake;
> Because Your mercy is good, deliver me.
>
> PSALM 109:21 NKJV

The Race

Can you hear the distant drums, do you hear the cries?
Can you see the clouds begin to darken in the skies?
Do you feel the earth beneath your feet begin to shake?
Do you know it's time to guard your heart and stay awake?

In every city, every town, in nations far and wide,
Hearts are being torn apart across the great divide.
Lives hang in the balance as the sand of time runs down,
So lift your eyes to heaven while there's mercy to be found.

For the day will come when we'll hear the trumpet sound,
And upon this earth Christ will stand.
So be strong and true, run the race He set for you,
For the kingdom of God is at hand.

Are you tired of the journey, are you growing cold?
Bring the embers of your fire to the Lamb of God.
Cast aside the things that pull you far away from home.
God will give a heart of flesh; He'll take your heart of stone.

For the day will come when we'll hear the trumpet sound,
And upon this earth Christ will stand.
So be strong and true, run the race He set for you,
For the kingdom of God is at hand.[3]

Stones of Mercy into Pools of Pain

The Beverly Hillbillies,
That's our name.
So much luggage,
The porter's lame.
One in a wheelchair,
One in a stroller,
One of us limping,
He leans on my shoulder.
But we're together—
For better or worse.
(I wonder if we can afford a full-time nurse?)

What a difference it made having William and Eleanor with us. Now when I was on stage, Christian was with his nana, and William could help Barry at our book table. (I got my revenge for the great kitchen redecoration. For that entire year of Women of Faith Conferences, William wore a sign around his neck: "I reorganized Sheila's kitchen." And I told the story from the stage so everyone could tease him about it!)

God has unexpected ways of throwing stones of mercy into pools of pain. There had never been a time in her life when Eleanor needed the fellowship and support of godly women more than now, and at that very moment she was enfolded into such a group. And there had never been a moment when I needed her so much, and she was there.

The six of us who make up the Women of Faith speaking team are a pretty tight bunch; we jealously guard our moments of privacy together. I say six, but it's really seven. You need to add Mary Graham. Our boss, our emcee at the conferences, our advocate in any difficult situation. It would be hard to put into words the kind of woman she is. The truest friend you could ever hope to find. Suffice it to say: Barry, Christian, and I love her body and soul. We would each donate one of our kidneys to her if she needed it. She brought Christian a stuffed elephant back from her latest trip to Africa, which he named Mary Graham. Thankfully, she took it as a compliment!

Our conferences run from Friday night through Saturday afternoon. The hour before we begin on Friday is sacred to us. All seven of us gather with Lana Bateman, our intercessor, and spend time before the throne of grace. Sometimes relatives or friends will join us for dinner at five, but when it's time for devotions, everyone leaves, and then we honestly, wholeheartedly throw ourselves before the Lord.

One night as Eleanor was leaving to take Christian for a walk around the arena in his stroller, I saw something in her eyes I couldn't ignore. A spiritual hunger. The silent cry of a drowning woman, praying that someone would throw her a line. So I asked my friends if they would consider letting Eleanor join us.

Perhaps it seems strange to you that we would be so keen to guard our privacy. It's just that our lives have become so public, we need a place where we can fall apart if we need to, a place to share the most personal details and struggles, a safe place. Yet when I asked them about Eleanor joining us, they all said yes. I didn't realize until Eleanor's final moments what a gift that had been.

Most of the time she would just listen. Sometimes she would cry silently. Sometimes she would pray, choking over her words of thanks that she was with good women in a good place. She would take the conference audiotapes home and listen to them over and over. She began to read her Bible more, finding comfort in the Psalms. She read one particular psalm over and over:

> *He who dwells in the shelter of the Most High*
> *   will rest in the shadow of the Almighty.*
> *I will say of the* LORD, *"He is my refuge and*
> *   my fortress,*
> *   my God, in whom I trust."*
> *Surely he will save you from the fowler's snare*
> *   and from the deadly pestilence.*
> *He will cover you with his feathers,*
> *   and under his wings you will find refuge;*
> *   his faithfulness will be your shield and rampart.*

You will not fear the terror of night,
>   nor the arrow that flies by day,
nor the pestilence that stalks in the darkness,
>   nor the plague that destroys at midday.
A thousand may fall at your side,
>   ten thousand at your right hand,
>   but it will not come near you.
You will only observe with your eyes
>   and see the punishment of the wicked.
If you make the Most High your dwelling—
>   even the LORD, who is my refuge—
then no harm will befall you,
>   no disaster will come near your tent.
For he will command his angels concerning you
>   to guard you in all your ways;
they will lift you up in their hands,
>   so that you will not strike your foot against a stone.
You will tread upon the lion and the cobra;
>   you will trample the great lion and the serpent.
"Because he loves me," says the LORD, "I will
>   rescue him;
I will protect him, for he acknowledges my name.
He will call upon me, and I will answer him;
>   I will be with him in trouble,
>   I will deliver him and honor him.
With long life will I satisfy him
>   and show him my salvation."

PSALM 91 NIV

One night as we sat around the kitchen table in our home in Nashville, Eleanor asked me, "Doesn't that sound to you as if God is going to heal me? It says no disaster will come near me. It says God will deliver me."

"It does, Mom," I answered, "and that's what we're going to believe."

Yet I've always struggled with healing. I know that God can heal anyone in a moment, yet He doesn't seem to do it a lot. I had wrestled with this constantly when I was cohost of *The 700 Club* on the Christian Broadcasting Network. We seemed to show only stories of those who were healed, and that made me realize that everyone else who sits at home, sick, wonders what he or she is doing wrong.

I guess my faith is weak. I long to be able to walk into a cancer ward, an AIDS hospice, a hospital for dying children, and see them all raised up miraculously. But I don't. At this point in my life, all I have to give is my presence—just to be there. I have sat with a friend in the last stages of full-blown AIDS and held his hand as Barry led him to Christ. I've wept with friends of mine in our small Bible study group at church as they buried their seven-month-old daughter. I live with so many questions, and yet I have seen grace soak us to the skin, even as a final breath leaves a human body.

Eleanor wanted to be healed and so we did all we knew to do. One of the conferences in 1998 was in Charlotte, North Carolina. We discovered that Mahesh Chavdah was conducting healing services at the same time as our Friday night meeting. I had interviewed Mahesh as a guest on *The 700 Club* and had tremendous respect for him. He seemed so normal to me compared to the theatrics I'd seen in others.

(NOTE TO READER: Theatrics are not my thing, but I would not for a moment suggest that God is not in things I don't understand.)

I called the church where Mahesh would be preaching. I told them I was speaking at the Coliseum that night and couldn't get there until about 11:00 P.M. They told me to come whenever I could, and he would still be there. After the conference Barry, William, and I went back to the hotel. William stayed with a sleeping Christian, and Barry, Eleanor, and I caught a cab to the church. We slipped into one of the back rows. Mahesh was still preaching.

I had only seen Barry cry a couple of times before. Once when Christian was born. Now Barry just sat with his head in his hands and wept; it broke my heart to see his pain for his mom. There is something sobering about the gift of life and the reality of death.

Then Mahesh invited anyone who wanted prayer to come to the altar. Eleanor went forward and knelt down. Barry and I knelt behind her. Mahesh came up to us. He asked Eleanor what was wrong. He brought his elders over and anointed her with oil, and then they blew the shofar trumpets, which have been blown since the beginning of Jewish history and are still blown in Israel today.

Please, God, oh, please heal her, I prayed.

It was about two in the morning when we got back to the hotel. Now we would have to wait for her doctor to run the cell count tests.

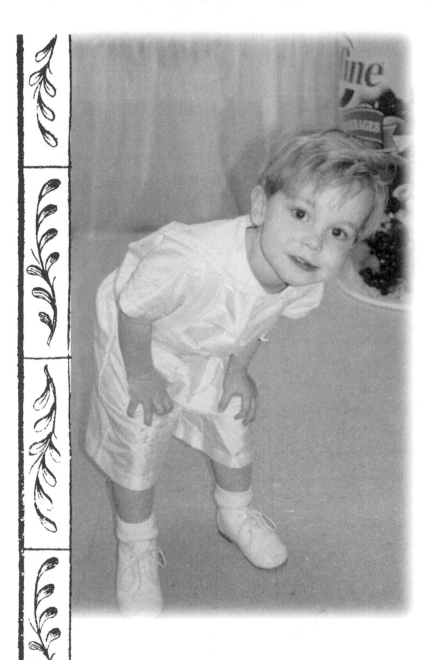

Pain in the Process

Have mercy on me, O LORD, for I am weak;
O LORD, heal me, for my bones are troubled.

PSALM 6:2 NKJV

We had a month off from touring, so William and Eleanor went to Charleston, and Barry, Christian, and I left for Nashville. You would think, you would hope, that when someone is dying it would bring out the best in all of us. It did not. The next few months were awful.

"I don't know why my mom gets so mad at me," Barry said one day at breakfast.

"What happened?"

"She wants to know every single thing we do every day. If I don't give her a detailed blow-by-blow account, she gets mad. I hate that!"

"She probably just wants to feel connected," I said. "Why don't I do that? I could fill her in on all our stuff."

"Great!" Barry said. "That's perfect. She'll love that."

So every time Eleanor called or I called Charleston to talk to her, I had a whole list of all we'd been doing: who we'd had over for dinner, what new clothes I had bought for Christian, what I was writing about. Then I'd listen as she told me anything that was new with her health, or how she felt, or what friends she'd seen that week. I thought we were doing great.

I was wrong.

One day in the spring of 1998 Barry answered the phone; it was his mom. From the other side of the room I could hear her yelling at him. But I had no clue what was going on. Finally I heard him say, "No, I won't pass you to Sheila. You need to calm down."

Once he hung up I asked, "What on earth was that about?"

"My mom's mad because she thinks you've put a wall up between her and me. She said she never gets to me anymore, that you've shut her out."

I was blown away. I had no idea that my attempt to provide Eleanor with all the little details of our lives would make her feel alienated from her son.

Then I got mad! All I could see was how unfair that seemed. I was trying to keep her in the loop, and now I was the enemy.

"Well, fine!" I said. "You talk to her from now on. I've had it!"

I took a cup of coffee out into the yard and watched the horses in my neighbor's field. We live in the country, just south of Nashville, and it's very peaceful. I ranted and raved at God for a while and then sat down under a tree. A few minutes later Christian came out with his bubbles.

"Look, Mommy!" he said. "Look at the colors when the sun hits the bubbles." His face was filled with simple joy. "I love you, Mommy," he said, planting a kiss on my nose.

As he ran off after Tom, our neighbor's cat, I thought of Eleanor. Barry was once her little boy, and she was leaving him much too soon. I left my pride in the grass and went inside and picked up the phone.

"Hi, Mom, it's me. I'm calling to say I'm sorry. I had no thought of keeping you from Barry. I was just trying to fill in the details he never gets to."

There was silence. Then I heard Eleanor crying. Finally she was able to talk. "I know I can be ugly sometimes, Sheila. I just wish Barry would talk to me more."

"I know," I said. "That's men for you! They just give you the bottom line . . . I love you, Mom, and Barry loves you so much."

"I love you, too, darling."

Lord, I don't have what it takes here. I want to be a channel of Your grace and mercy, but I get so mad sometimes. Please, please help me. Help me rush into Your presence and live there.

The Test Results

My tears have been my
food day and night,
while men say to me all day long,
"Where is your God?" . . .
Why are you downcast, O my soul?
Why so disturbed within me?
Put your hope in God,
for I will yet praise him,
my Savior and my God.

PSALM 42:3, 5 NIV

*I*n the summer of 1998 we received the test results: the cancer cells had doubled. It didn't look good. Eleanor opted not
to take any more chemotherapy. She wasn't in pain, but she was
weak and tired at times.

"Mom, I think you need to stop traveling with us now. It's too
much for you," I said one day when we were visiting them in
Charleston.

"Sheila, what do you think I'd rather do? Sit here at home
dying a little more each day, or be out with the people I love?"

I said no more. She did well for eighteen months. And
Christian was an amazing source of comfort to her. He was a

normal, rowdy kid, almost two years old at that time, but with Eleanor he was soft and sweet, as if he understood. He would lie in bed with her and pat her face and say, "Nana, you're beautiful!"

Those last months on the road were a patchwork quilt of tears and laughter, of sweet words and verbal bullets. Pain squeezed my soul till I could scream. There were nights when Barry and I would get back to the hotel after twelve hours of talking and listening to the women who wanted a moment to share their own story, and Eleanor would smile and listen and regale us with Christian's antics. Other nights she would tell us that we were trying to kill her. Dying must make you feel so alone.

I wrote a lot during those difficult days. I spilled my hopes and dreams, my faith and unbelief, into my laptop. One of the hardest moments was during a trip to Charleston when Eleanor asked me if I thought God was punishing her. I could have wept that that thought even sat with her for a moment. I held her for a while and cried with her. Then I picked up my Bible and read her these words:

Who shall separate us from the love of Christ? Shall trouble or hardship or persecution or famine or nakedness or danger or sword? As it is written:

> *"For your sake we face death all day long;*
> *we are considered as sheep to be slaughtered."*

No, in all these things we are more than conquerors through him who loved us. For I am convinced that neither death nor life, neither angels nor demons, neither the present nor the future, nor any powers, neither height nor depth, nor anything else in all creation, will be able to separate us from the love of God that is in Christ Jesus our Lord.

ROMANS 8:35–39 NIV

There were moments when these words were comforting to her, and moments when they seemed untrue. God could heal her. He appeared to be choosing not to.

Blue Waters

Oh my soul, remember . . .
I know that my God never sleeps;
Day and night He watches over me.
Lift my eyes unto Him.
All my help comes from the Lord;
Remember all His faithfulness to me.

Holy, holy, my Redeemer
In blue waters washes me;
Holy, holy God, my Healer,
Catches every tear I cry.

Oh my soul, remember,
Remember all that His love can do;
Remember all His faithfulness to you.

Holy, holy, my Redeemer
In blue waters washes me;
Holy, holy God, my Healer,
Catches every tear I cry.

You will never let my steps be moved
And I will rest completely in Your love.[4]
—FROM THE BLUE WATERS ALBUM

Our Last Christmas

For to us a child is born, to us a son is given,
 and the government will be on his shoulders.
And he will be called
Wonderful Counselor, Mighty God,
Everlasting Father, Prince of Peace.

ISAIAH 9:6 NIV

I think we all knew it would be Eleanor's last Christmas. It had been almost two years from the time the doctor gave her the prognosis of six months to two years. We all wanted it to be the best holiday ever. William and Eleanor were coming to visit us for a month.

I decorated the house like a crazed Christmas elf. We had two trees, one live and one artificial, all fourteen feet of it. We placed wreaths with big red bows on every window. A huge wreath, laden with fruit and angels and pinecones and so big you could hardly shut the door, hung on our front door. I had papier-mâché choirboys standing on Eleanor's bedside table. We bought a hand-painted, life-size Santa Claus for the front porch, and Bing Crosby daily belted out the old favorites.

I even attempted to make Christmas cookies in the shape of the star of Bethlehem—but they looked more like fried eggs.

Under the tree were presents galore. The pendant watch Mom had wanted for a while. A Christmas sweater from Christian. Her favorite cologne from the cats. I found out where there was a living Nativity scene to visit and anything else I could think of to make the holiday special.

Yet Christmas was a disaster!

Now I know why, but I didn't understand then. All I could see was that Eleanor seemed to be mad at me the whole time. She hardly came out of her room. She didn't want to do anything. She lay in bed, watching television by herself.

"Are you okay, Mom?" I asked. "Are you in pain?"

"No. I just want to be left alone."

Then for two days she wouldn't talk to me at all. She would come through the living room into the kitchen and sit at the breakfast table. She would talk to William, to Christian, to Barry, to the cats—but Eleanor completely ignored me. She wouldn't answer anything I asked her.

By the second day of that, I had had it! Barry found me in the closet in my bedroom in tears.

"I don't know what else to do," I said. "I don't even know what I've done."

That day Barry and his mom had a heart-to-heart, and it got very heated; I know, because Christian and I were in the next room where I was reading him a bedtime story. Eleanor's voice got louder and louder.

"Is Nana cross?" he asked.

"Yes," I replied. "Nana doesn't feel so good. You know how a booboo can make you cry?"

"Yes," he said.

"This is just Nana's way of crying."

"Sure is loud!"

Somehow we got through that Christmas holiday. The day before the Pfaehlers left, it was just Eleanor and me in the kitchen.

"Mom, I know that you must be afraid. It's okay to be angry, but please tell me how you're feeling. If I'm hurting you in some way, tell me. It's the last thing I want to do."

"I just wanted this Christmas to be different," she said. "I just wanted to talk. I wanted us all to sit down and talk, but you had all this Christmas stuff arranged and people coming around."

"I thought that's what you wanted."

"Not this year."

We held each other and wept.

The next day Barry took his parents to the airport with Christian. When he came back, I could tell he had been crying.

"Are you okay, babe?" I asked.

"Mom stood at the door going into the terminal for a couple of minutes and just looked at me," he said. "I know she'll never be back here again."

Let His Love Flow Down

If you knew your end was near,
If your final song was here,
What would it be?
If you'd one thing you could say
Before your world was swept away,
What would it be?
If you had to take it all,
All the moments, great and small,
And leave a single sentence for the world?

When all is said and done,
What's the message of the Son?
Let His love, let His love flow down.

Let His love flow down like a river;
Let the healing stream start to run.
From the heart of the Lamb through
    the hands of His children,
Let His love, let His love flow down.

As we see the end is near,
And the Lamb is almost here to take us home,
As we wait to see His face,
We are channels of His grace and love alone.

So let's live with heart and soul,
See each child as precious gold,
The image of our Father here on earth.

When all is said and done,
What's the message of the Son?
Let His love, let His love flow down.

Let His love flow down like a river;
Let the healing stream start to run.
From the heart of the Lamb through
      the hands of His children,
Let His love, let His love flow down.[5]

The Long Road Home

You prepare a table before me in the presence
  of my enemies.
You anoint my head with oil;
  my cup overflows.
Surely goodness and love will follow me
  all the days of my life,
and I will dwell in the house of the LORD forever.

PSALM 23:5–6 NIV

leanor never traveled again. At the beginning of January 1999, she told us that her time with Women of Faith was over. I understood; I couldn't believe she'd made it so long. After that she went down fast.

Whenever we weren't on the road, we tried to be with her. She could still go for a ride in the car with William—but not too far or for too long. Most of the time she slept on the sofa in the den, surrounded by Barry memorabilia. She now had hospice care.

One day in February William called. "I think you'd better come. The nurse says that all her organs are closing down."

We were on the next flight to Charleston and arrived at 11:00 P.M. By the time we got to the house, Christian was fast asleep. I put him in our bed, and Barry and I climbed up the stairs to her room. Eleanor lay very still. She looked pale and thin. Her hair was brushed back from her face, and I noticed that her fingernails were growing out under her artificial nails. It seemed like such a silly thing to notice when she was being ravaged by liver cancer, but I knew it would have bothered her. And for me it was a small distraction from the pain and helplessness I was feeling; this was something I could control, something I could do for her. (Later I called her nail technician and asked if she would come out to the house, which she did.) Fans were blowing in her face.

"It's cold in here, Pop," I said.

"That's the way she likes it . . . She feels hot. She has a fever."

Barry sat on the edge of the bed and took her hand. "Mom . . . Mom. It's me, Barry."

Eleanor opened her eyes. "Oh Barry, it's you. I'm so glad you're here."

He kissed her cheek. "Sheila's here too."

I sat on the other side of the bed and kissed her forehead. "Hi, Mom!"

"Hello, darling," she said and smiled.

The four of us talked for two hours. Eleanor told us about how she felt when she knew she was pregnant with Barry. We laughed at how they spoiled him. "Buying that red Camaro was the ruining of you!" she teased.

We talked about Christian and her eyes filled with tears. "I'll miss that sweet boy. I'll never get to see him grow up or ride a bike or take him shopping just by himself."

We all wept. And we laughed.

"Mom, remember the time you and Dad stayed at our first

apartment when we were out of town? You ordered Domino's Pizza. I had told you the code to open the gate to the apartment complex, but you forgot. Our telephone recorded your conversation with the pizza driver on our machine! Remember?"

When Eleanor and William weren't sure they did, I gave them my own version of the dialog:

Delivery Man: Hello, this is Domino's Pizza.

William: Oh, yes. Come in.

Delivery Man: Sir, you need to enter the code to open the gate.

William: The code! Oh, Lord! Mama, do you remember the code?

Eleanor: What code?

William: Oh, Lord. We're from Charleston!

Delivery Man: That doesn't help me much, sir. Do you want your pizza?

William: Hang on a minute. I'll run to the gate.

We all laughed at my rendition. Then I reminded William, "By the time you got back, you were exhausted, and your pizza was cold." Again we laughed at the memory, such a sweet blessing in this moment of pain.

Then William and I left Barry alone with his mom for a while, and we went to check on Christian. He was tucked up snugly, fast asleep, his round cherub face looking so peaceful and innocent. When we returned, Barry's dad said, "Let's let her sleep now, and we will see where we are in the morning."

Christian slept between Barry and me that night. About five o'clock in the morning he got up, and I heard him say, "Mommy, I'm off to see Nana . . . bye."

I called after him, "No, no, wait for Mommy." I didn't know if Eleanor had made it through the night, and I didn't want Christian to walk in on that. But he was way ahead of me, running up the stairs. I grabbed my robe and ran after him. By the time I got upstairs, he was standing right beside her bed. William was sitting on the edge. Eleanor was very still. Her eyes were closed.

"Nana?" Christian said.

She didn't respond.

"Nana, it's me, Christian . . . Nana?"

In that moment she opened her eyes.

"Well, hello! There you are!" Christian crawled into bed beside her and gave her a big kiss.

By that evening Eleanor was downstairs eating dinner with us!

The next day the nurse said, "In my twenty-two years of hospice work, I have never seen anyone so close to death—where everything is closing down—turn around and come back."

To me it was an example of the power of love to call us from death to life. Eleanor was definitely close to home, so close it was as if you could see the spray of the River Jordan on her face. But she heard that little voice and turned around and came back.

Since then I've wondered how often we live our lives that way. We just go along, looking okay, but we are dead inside. If we could only stop long enough to hear God's voice saying, "Hello, hello!" And then open our eyes, as Eleanor did, and hear God saying, "Well, there you are!"

Instead we rush through our lives, not listening to God's quiet voice calling us back to Himself. We know He said, "I've come to give you life. Not existence, not just getting through one more day, I've come to give you life, and all it holds."

If only we'd stop and listen.

We thought we would lose Eleanor that weekend, but God gifted us with a few more months.

Mental note: Stop and really look at my family and friends—beyond what seems to be true to what is real.

A Time to Laugh
and a Time to Cry

There is a time for everything,
and a season for every activity under heaven:
a time to be born and a time to die,
a time to plant and a time to uproot,
a time to kill and a time to heal,
a time to tear down and a time to build,
a time to weep and a time to laugh,
a time to mourn and a time to dance,
a time to scatter stones and a time to gather them,
a time to embrace and a time to refrain,
a time to search and a time to give up,
a time to keep and a time to throw away,
a time to tear and a time to mend,
a time to be silent and a time to speak,
a time to love and a time to hate,
a time for war and a time for peace.

ECCLESIASTES 3:1–8 NIV

*O*ne of our last pictures

of Eleanor

Broken Dreams and Unexpected Graces

> Have mercy on me, O LORD, for I am in trouble;
> My eye wastes away with grief,
> Yes, my soul and my body!
>
> PSALM 31:9 NKJV

Two months before Eleanor died, we were off the road so we could be in Charleston with her. I have so many memories. It was a most unusual time. I can't think of a greater privilege than walking the final mile of someone's journey with them. It will change you forever.

Toward the end we had to move her to a hospital bed in her room upstairs. We tried to persuade her to be downstairs, because it would be easier for everyone. But she wanted to be up in her room, surrounded by the marvelous doll collection she had gathered for the last twenty-five years.

Because Eleanor's final homegoing went on for eight weeks, Barry, William, and I would relieve each other. One of us would sit upstairs for four or five hours while the others caught a nap or ran errands. Eleanor did not want to die. She was ready to die and accepted that it was going to happen, but she wasn't an eighty-year-old woman who wanted to go home. She was a sixty-seven-year-old woman with a two-and-a-half-year-old grandson, Christian. The fact that she knew she was going to die was a broken dream.

In the midst of that broken dream, there were so many unexpected graces. She and I were both changed by her dying process. We learned to listen. We learned to give and receive love and to tell the truth to each other. We were both better women as the end neared. Only God could have done that.

Throughout her last days I tried to make sure I allowed Christian to be with her as much as possible. But half of me was afraid. *How much am I supposed to protect him as his mother?* I wondered. *And how much am I supposed to get out of the way and let this grandmother have her last moments with her grandchild?*

The balance was hard to find.

One day Christian said, "Nana's sick, Mommy?"

"Yes, darling, Nana's sick."

"Does she have a booboo?"

"Yes, baby," I replied. "Nana has a big booboo."

"I could help," he said.

"What do you mean?"

Christian pulled his *Arthur* book out of his backpack and then I understood. Arthur is a character from one of Christian's favorite PBS television shows. The book he pulled out was on booboos. I knew what he wanted, so I got him into his car seat, and we drove to the drugstore. I led him to the First Aid section.

"You pick them out, Christian," I said. "Get the ones you want."

He reached up and took a large tin of bandages with cartoon characters on them. He could hardly wait to get them to Nana, so as soon as we arrived home, he went straight up to her room.

"Nana?" he asked. "Where is your booboo?"

I leaned over and whispered Dr. Christian's plans for treatment in her ear.

"Right here, darling," she said, pointing to her left hand where there was a mark left by an I.V. drip.

Christian reached into his box and took out a bandage with Goofy on it. He carefully applied it to her hand.

"Thank you, Christian," she said. "That's much better."

That became his pattern. Every morning and every evening Eleanor was graced with another Disney character. What a sport she was. She was covered in them. She looked like a dying tourist.

Until about a week before she died, Christian liked to get in bed with her and lie down beside her. He was now a rowdy, jumping, screaming, full of life two-and-a-half-year-old boy, but as I've said, he had an unusual sensitivity to her.

One night when Eleanor's feet were hurting, I gave her a kind of pedicure. I bought some lotion and rubbed her feet. Then I cut her toenails.

"Why don't I paint your toenails, Eleanor?" I asked.

She nodded her agreement. I got red polish and painted her toenails. Then I took the covers off her feet because she felt the pressure was too much. Later that night, when Christian came up to kiss her good night, he kissed her cheek and said, "I love you, Nana, and I think your toenails are beautiful."

I hadn't told him I'd given her a pedicure. He just noticed all by himself. (To any three-year-old girl reading this book, we are talking good husband material here!)

The next day Christian wanted to take a nap with Nana. I

could tell that she was a lot worse. Every breath seemed to be an effort. At times she would hold her breath for several seconds.

At first I said, "I don't think that's a good idea, darling. Nana is really tired."

"But I want to," he said. "Nana likes it when I take a nap with her."

So I made a deal. "Why doesn't Mommy come, too, and we can all have a nap?"

"That's cool!" he answered.

The two of us got into the hospital bed with Eleanor, with me in the middle. I was holding Eleanor's hand and Christian's hand. They both fell asleep. Eleanor was very thin now. She had lost fifty pounds. Her red hair, which had never seen a drop of dye in her life, was pushed back from her forehead. She was wearing a red gown the color of her hair. She had no makeup on and her face was soft, like a little girl's. I could see the morphine patch on her chest and the nitroglycerin patch for her heart beside it.

I had to be careful I didn't lie on her catheter, which had taken the nurse and me fifteen minutes to get in; I didn't want to put Eleanor through that again. We'd had to cut her nightgowns up the back so we could change her without hurting her. Christian was in the little clown pajamas we had bought when Mary Graham, Ney Bailey (Mary's roommate and our dear friend), and Barry and I had gone to see the Cirque Du Soliel show during our last trip to Florida. Christian had his head on my breast, his brown–blond hair curling around his ears.

They were both in diapers. I had just changed Eleanor's and I had just changed Christian's. I lay there looking at both of them with tears rolling down my face. And I thought, *Lord, what is our purpose in life? Between the moment when we come into this world, vulnerable and helpless, dependent on someone else for everything, like Christian, and the moment when we are so close to home and are once again helpless and dependent, like Eleanor? What is our purpose? What's the highest calling, the best we can be? What makes You happy?*

At that moment I felt an overwhelming rush of an answer: The only purpose of our life is to learn to love God and be a conduit of that love to those around us. I thought of all the time Eleanor and I had wasted on stupid stuff that didn't matter at all. I thought of how we both had treated each day so casually, as if it had no real value in itself, never knowing if this might be our last day together.

I remembered again a lesson I thought I'd learned, but that had been devoured by my own sinful nature: The whole purpose of my life is to become more like Christ. Therefore everything—that would be everything—that comes into it, good or bad, can be used by Him to make me into the woman He has called me to be. Stupid arguments with my mother-in-law, canceled flights, long lines in grocery stores, illness—everything can be viewed as a gift.

Mental note: Have my brain checked for leakage.

An Immaculate Conception?

They shall utter the memory of Your great goodness,
And shall sing of Your righteousness.

PSALM 145:7 NKJV

*O*ne night in March, Barry and I sat with Eleanor for three or
four hours. When she was conscious, we would talk to her
about Christian. We talked about all the fun things we'd done together. We remembered our trip to Disney World and Christian's
face when he met Mickey Mouse. Eleanor smiled at the wonderful memories.

After that she seemed to go to sleep, and she looked peaceful.
Barry and I were talking about how glad we were that she now
seemed to have peace that Christian wouldn't ever forget her.
Barry had tears in his eyes.

Suddenly Eleanor sat up in bed and grabbed both of our hands.
"Call the doctor," she cried.

"Mom, I'll call him," I said. "But . . . are you in pain again?"

"No," she answered. "I think I'm pregnant."

"Mom," I replied. "If you are pregnant, there is a star in the
East, and three wise men are coming down the Savannah Highway right now."

Then Eleanor laid back against her pillow and passed out again.

Neither Barry nor I could keep from chuckling. An unexpected gift of laughter in the midst of a broken dream.

Eleanor and Christian wearing
bunny glasses

Compassion: The Child of Joy and Sorrows

Now we know the end is near
And the Lamb is almost here to take you home.
As you wait to see His face,
We are channels of His grace and love alone.

So let's live with heart and soul
See each day as precious gold,
The greatest gift from Father here on earth.

When all is said and done,
What's the message of the Son?
Let His love, let His love flow down.

*O*ne day toward the end Eleanor was in a lot of pain. We were now giving her morphine every two hours. As I sat with her that particular day, I played a tape of some of her favorite hymns. She was holding my hand tightly, so I could tell she was hurting. I felt helpless. I'd given her as much pain medication as the nurse said I could, but I decided that when William or Barry came up to relieve me, I was going to call the nurse. As far as I was concerned, there was no way Eleanor should be in pain if there was anything we could do.

Then she said to me, "How much longer, Sheila? How much longer is this going to be? If God is going to take me, why can't He just take me now? Why does it have to be so hard?"

"I don't know, Mom," I said as I gathered her in my arms. "I don't know why it has to be this way. We will do everything we can to relieve you of this pain."

Just at that moment I looked out the window behind her bed, and I could see and hear Christian. He was running around playing in the backyard, trying to find the neighbor's cat. Then he stopped at a bush and stooped to peer inside the branches. I could vaguely see the outline of the poor cat, crouched among the leaves.

"Listen, cat," Christian said. "Come here! Yes, you! You come here now or you'll get a time-out! I mean it, cat. There will be no lunch; there will be nothing for you if you don't get out here this very minute. I'm not kidding, cat!"

I was holding my mother-in-law, who was in pain, and my heart was with her. Yet at the same time I was watching my darling little boy and laughing with him. What a strange moment. Joy and sorrow at the same time. The child playing with a cat, just an ordinary day in his life. And the grandmother struggling with the pain of dying.

I used to think I was either going through a time of joy—and there were no shadows there—or I was going through a time of tremendous sorrow—and there was no daylight. After walking with Eleanor through her final journey, I believe that for the rest of my life I will walk hand in hand with both of those realities. At the same moments I know joy, I will also be aware of sorrow.

How can we live in this battered, broken world and not ache? Yet how can we turn our face toward home and not dance? It's almost as if those parents, joy and sorrow, give birth to compassion. When we walk with both, God changes the way we view life and the way we view people.

I used to be so afraid around sick or dying people. I thought, *What if I don't say the right thing?* Then I finally got it. There *is* no right thing to say. What can we possibly say that makes any of the pain all right? Yet we can bring the presence of Christ to each other. As the Scripture says, "we have this treasure in jars of clay to show that this all-surpassing power is from God and not from us" (2 Cor. 4:7 NIV).

So my new prayer is simply this: "Lord, rise up in me! Touch Your people. Fill this earthen vessel, which will never be any more than that, with Yourself—for Your name's sake!"

God doesn't use us because we've had a good day. He uses us for His own name's sake. It is who He is!

In her dying Eleanor found what she had longed for in living. Peace, rest, intimacy, the ability to receive. Before that time, it had been very hard for her to receive; she was very much a giver. Whenever she came to our house, she would cook and do the laundry, as I've mentioned before. She would do, do, do—until she was exhausted.

During her last precious weeks, I talked to her about some of the misunderstandings we had in our time together. We talked about that last Christmas, where we missed one another and didn't connect at all. I realized that sometimes she had said the exact opposite of what she wanted. She was so afraid. She prayed that I would be able to hear beyond what she was saying and know what she really meant. She wanted me to hear, "Please hold me," when what she said was, "Leave me alone." In my own pride, or in my own inability to get the bigger picture, I didn't hear what she was really saying. As she admitted this to me, I finally understood. So often I use anger as a shield for my fear.

"All the times I told you that you never loved me, I knew you did," Eleanor said.

I laid my head down on her lap and cried as she gently stroked my hair.

We both received grace in those moments. Moments when you can't talk. Moments when you are on holy ground. Moments when you both let go and are swimming in the deep blue waters of the grace of God.

The Book of Joy and Sorrow

Open to me words of wisdom in the midst of life's dark days.
Take away my human blindness, give me eyes to see Your ways.
I am weak without Your goodness, I am lost without Your light.
Word of God, sweet breath of heaven,
      shine upon this child tonight.

Open to me words of kindness when my heart is sad within.
Help me rise above the sorrow, singing songs of joy again.
I will lift my voice to worship,
      thankful for Your gift of grace.
Word of peace, sweet breath of heaven—
      friend, until I see your face.

Open now the halls of heaven to each child who seeks Your face.
Mercy flowing like a river from the Christ who took our place.
Took our guilt and shame upon Him, bore our pain upon the tree.
Word of life, sweet breath of heaven, Love of every love to me.[6]

Black Comedy

There was a young boy—yes, he's mine—
Who was funny without really trying.
He grabbed the remote,
Thought his grandma could float.
And said, "Oh look, Nana's flying!"

Some of the last moments of Eleanor's life were both funny and painful, like the night we were trying to figure out just how much morphine she needed to manage the pain. We could not increase her dosage until the hospice nurse got back to us, and we'd been waiting for the nurse to return our call for fifteen minutes. That may not seem long to you or me, but when a loved one is in pain with cancer, it's an eternity.

Barry went to the store to fill a prescription, and William and I decided to give Eleanor a pill to help her sleep. But we were having trouble getting her to swallow anything, never mind a pill. It was a disaster.

"Okay, here's how we will do this," William said to me. "You hold this flashlight and shine it in her face. I'll get her to stick her tongue out, and I'll put the pill on her tongue. Then I'll try to push it to the back of her mouth and make sure that it goes down."

This didn't sound clinically correct to me, but I knew Eleanor needed help.

At that point Christian came upstairs and saw me holding the flashlight. He also saw the remote control on the side of Eleanor's hospital bed and began pushing it up and down. He thought it was a game.

"Look at Nana," he said. "Yahoo! This is fun. Look at Nana go! She's flying!!"

The bed was going up and down, and the pill we had so carefully placed on her tongue went flying across the room. Fortunately, amazingly, Eleanor had finally fallen asleep; she didn't seem to know what was going on!

I dropped the flashlight and grabbed the pill before Christian thought it was candy. William and I laughed so hard we had tears

rolling down our faces. We had to sit down or we would have fallen down. Of course, Christian joined in our laughter! It was one of those light moments in the midst of pressure, strain, and grief, a moment when you get a second to catch your breath before the next battle.

Finally the hospice nurse called. "Eleanor can't swallow any more," she said. "So from now on we'll up the dosage on her morphine patch and give any additional medicine intravenously."

I didn't tell the nurse about the show she missed!

$\mathcal{S}$heila in $\mathcal{S}$cotland

Prayers We Didn't Know to Pray

And when you pray, do not be like the hypocrites, for they love to pray standing in the synagogues and on the street corners to be seen by men. I tell you the truth, they have received their reward in full. But when you pray, go into your room, close the door and pray to your Father, who is unseen. Then your Father, who sees what is done in secret, will reward you.

And when you pray, do not keep on babbling like pagans, for they think they will be heard because of their many words. Do not be like them, for your Father knows what you need before you ask him.

MATTHEW 6:5–8 NIV

The disciples were so right when they asked Jesus to teach them to pray. We all prayed, "God, heal her." Eleanor went to all sorts of healing meetings, even one in the final month at her own church. I think it was one of those strange paradoxes of the kingdom of God that our prayers were answered in ways we did not expect: the peace she found in the last moments of her life, the intimacy with her family, and the joy that she is now experiencing in finally being home. God healed her in ways much greater than she or I could ever have put into words.

Eleanor and I found joy with tear-stained faces. I began to see how caught up we are in the "now," in what we think will make us happy this minute. We run around like squirrels, gathering stuff, never stopping, wondering why we don't feel loved.

I've decided to change the way I pray. I used to pray with a whole long list of things I wanted God to do; now I pray for wisdom, and I pray to be more like Christ. My friend Marilyn Meberg once asked Orville Swindoll, Luci's big brother, "What is the most important thing you learned during your life on the mission field?" I love his reply: "I used to think the most important thing was to be right. Now I know it's to become like Jesus Christ."

Amen, Orville.

What joy!

Joy

There's a joy that's deep inside me
    that's stronger than the sun.
There's a peace that stays beside me,
    where'er the river runs.
There's a hope that's deep as midnight,
    that shines through any storm,
And a love that gently leads me
    on the path that takes me home.
This joy that I've been given,
This peace, this song of heaven,
This hope within my soul is burning,
And this love that leads me home.

There's nothing I can do,
There's nothing I can say,
That would make my poor heart worthy,
So I come through Christ, the Way.[7]

Final Requests

Let me sit in the sun,
Let me hold my head high,
Let me feel I'm alive once more till I die.

Two weeks before Eleanor died, she was completely unable to get out of bed. She was catheterized so she didn't have to worry about using a commode. She wasn't eating at all, so each time we changed her diaper it was usually clean. My big concern was that she would get bedsores, so every three hours William and Barry and I would turn her and prop pillows under her arms and knees and feet. I found a wonderful herbal lotion that I could rub on her back, legs, and feet, which seemed to help for a while.

One day as I looked at her, I noticed how stringy and unkempt her lovely red hair was. "We need to try and wash your mom's hair," I said to Barry. "She can't be comfortable with it like that."

We waited for the day nurse to come in and check her blood sugar level; Eleanor also suffered from severe diabetes. Then I asked the nurse if she would help me.

"We have a powder that's easy to use if you want to try that," she said.

"No, let's wash her hair. I'm sure she'll feel better."

What a carrying-on that was! But we managed. Barry and the nurse turned her sideways and supported her head off the pillow so I was able to wash and condition her hair. We wrapped it in a towel to get most of the water off, and then I brushed her hair dry.

"You smell like a princess, Mom!" I said.

She grabbed hold of my hand. "Thank you, darling!"

I was so glad I was able to give her this piece of comfort and dignity.

A couple of days later Eleanor surprised Barry and me when she said, "I want to get out of this bed one more time."

William was worried. "There's no way! She's very weak. We'll hurt her."

"Pop, we need to do this for her," I said. "She is dying. This is what she wants. If she wanted to go to the beach, I'd take her."

Barry agreed. He went downstairs and brought one of the cream-colored, wing-backed chairs, which stood in the den on either side of the sofa. Then he and I carried Eleanor as gently as we could. We made a human chair by placing one of our arms under her arm and our other arm under her knees. Then we carefully settled her in the soft, wing-backed chair.

Just before we had come to Charleston this last time, I had gone to the nicest lingerie store in Nashville and asked for their prettiest robe set. I gave them Eleanor's size, and the clerk and I found a lovely, pale green one, which I thought would be pretty with her red hair.

I got that out of her drawer, cut it up the back, and slipped it on. Then I brushed her hair and put a little makeup on her.

"Mom, you look beautiful," I said. "Is there anything else you'd like?"

"I'd like to see Bobbie," she said. "I'd like her to come for tea."

Bobbie Livingston was Mom's best friend. They had a deep empathy for one another, since Bobbie had lost her husband two years before and Eleanor had held her hand through that time. Now she wanted Bobbie's hand.

And Bobbie was quick to respond. When we called her, she said she would be there in five minutes. Barry went downstairs to the den and brought up the other wing-backed chair. When Bobbie arrived, we decided to leave them alone for a while. As I left the room I turned to look back. There they sat, side by side, holding hands. It was beautiful. One of those lovely moments, an unexpected grace.

About an hour later I went back upstairs. There they still were, holding hands, side by side, sitting in those high-backed chairs. Two Christian women, sisters in Christ, sharing their lives together. I asked Mom if I could get them anything.

"I think we would like a little soup," she said.

"Yes, ma'am!" I replied. I was thrilled. Eleanor hadn't eaten in about a week.

William and I got some chicken noodle soup and took it up in two china bowls. Bobbie fed it to Eleanor, and we were surprised that she ate it all.

From that moment on, she was never out of her bed again. This moment of friendship was a final gift of grace that God gave her in her last days. She came alive for those two hours in a way we had not seen in weeks. And when we got her settled back in bed again, she slept for ten hours, without moving, from the exhaustion of it all.

That afternoon as I walked Bobbie to her car, I said, "This must be so hard for you, Bobbie."

"I don't think I can bear it! . . . What will I do without her?"

We hugged for a long time, then she got into her car and backed out of the driveway. I felt that the next time I would see her would be at Eleanor's funeral.

Worship

Great is Thy faithfulness!
Great is Thy faithfulness, Lord, unto me!
—THOMAS O. CHISHOLM

J knew we were close to the end. Eleanor was not awake much anymore. It was hard to get her to sip even a little water, so sometimes we would put tiny ice chips on her lips. But she still surprised me! When I was by myself with her, I would read the Psalms or sing to her or play a favorite tape that Lana, our Women of Faith intercessor, brought when she came to sit with us through those last days. Eleanor loved the song "Come Rest a While" from an old Fisher folk album, so much so that Barry took it to a studio and put it on a loop so it would play over and over again. The lyrics were soft and tender.

The hospice nurse had told us, "Even when you think she's sleeping or so weak she can't hear, she can hear you. Even if she's not responding, know that she is taking in a lot." So as I would read the Twenty-third Psalm or sing a well-known hymn, I would suddenly see a smile on Eleanor's face.

One night at about two or three in the morning, I was sitting by her bed, holding her hand. I wasn't even watching her face. I had my eyes closed, and I was quietly singing "Great Is Thy Faithfulness." Suddenly I heard her join in:

Great is Thy faithfulness, Oh, God my Father,
There is no shadow of turning with Thee;
Thou changest not, Thy compassions, they fail not;
As Thou hast been, Thou forever wilt be.

Great is Thy faithfulness!
Great is Thy faithfulness!
Morning by morning new mercies I see;
All I have needed Thy hand hath provided—
Great is Thy faithfulness, Lord, unto me![8]

She sang that first verse and the chorus, and then she went back to sleep. I lay facedown on the floor. I was in unknown territory, a moment between life and death. I wept for an hour.

This holy moment made me realize something: you never know who is listening. Sometimes women sing as they work around the house or tell their family about their faith, and the response makes them think, *Nobody is paying any attention. Nobody here is joining with me in my faith.* They are worried about their kids or something that has happened, and they feel so alone. I say, "Keep on singing—someone may be listening; they just don't seem to be."

That moment in the middle of the night was holy, just like the sacred instance in the prophet Isaiah's life when he was allowed to glimpse beyond the veil.

> *In the year that King Uzziah died, I saw the Lord seated on*
> *a throne, high and exalted, and the train of his robe filled*

the temple. Above him were seraphs, each with six wings: With two wings they covered their faces, with two they covered their feet, and with two they were flying. And they were calling to one another:

> *"Holy, holy, holy is the LORD Almighty;*
> *the whole earth is full of his glory."*

At the sound of their voices the doorposts and thresholds shook and the temple was filled with smoke.

"Woe to me!" I cried. "I am ruined! For I am a man of unclean lips, and I live among a people of unclean lips, and my eyes have seen the King, the LORD Almighty."

Then one of the seraphs flew to me with a live coal in his hand, which he had taken with tongs from the altar. With it he touched my mouth and said, "See, this has touched your lips; your guilt is taken away and your sin atoned for."

Then I heard the voice of the Lord saying, "Whom shall I send? And who will go for us?" And I said, "Here am I. Send me!"

ISAIAH 6:1–8 NIV

Watching Eleanor die, and yet hearing her sing of the great faithfulness of God in the midst of the pain, was like a tornado blowing through my life, decimating my selfish heart. This moment marked my soul eternally. I wanted to want the things that mattered. *Here am I,* I thought. *Send me!*

Eleanor

Lay your tired golden head upon this pillow, dear.
There are angels watching over you,
And the Morning Star is in the heavens, close to you.

Can you see the moon shining in your room,
Tying golden ribbons in your hair?
May your sleep be sweet until the sun brings morning here.

And I never knew such a tender love
That could break my heart in two,
So I lie down gently now at Jesus' feet with you.

And I feel I'm lying on holy ground,
Such a gift God gave us in you.
So I kiss your fragile cheek and say a prayer for you.

Lay your tired golden head upon this pillow, dear.
There are angels watching over you,
And the Morning Star is in the heavens, close to you.

A Conversation Before Dying

Hear my cry for mercy as I call to you for help,
as I lift up my hands
toward your Most Holy Place.

PSALM 28:2 NIV

It was very quiet in her room. The only noise was the gentle whirring of a fan, like a summer dragonfly. Eleanor seemed to be sleeping. I sat beside her bed and took her hand in mine. It felt cold. Her face was thin and pale. At times she would hold her breath and I would count . . . 1-2-3-4-5-6-7-8-9. I found myself holding my breath, too, wondering if she would find her way back again.

That day, when I counted to twenty-one, I panicked. "Mom! Mom! Are you all right?"

She opened her eyes. "Hi, Sheila."

"Are you thirsty, Mom? Would you like a sip of ginger ale?" I asked as I leaned over her to brush the hair off her forehead.

"That would be good," she whispered.

I poured some of the soft drink into a plastic cup, put in a straw, and held the cup up to her dry lips. She took two swallows and pulled away.

"Are you in pain, Mom?"

She shook her head and closed her eyes.

"Mom, I want to ask you something." I paused for a moment, wondering if I was doing the right thing. Yet I was as sure as you can be when there is no choice that seems to be good. "Do you want to talk about when you die?"

Lana Bateman had encouraged me to broach this painful subject with Eleanor. Lana had walked the same road with her mother-in-law. "Many people will walk with you in your living," she had said. "Not many will walk with you in your dying."

Yet now that I had spoken the dreaded words, I was afraid it would make Eleanor feel as if I were hurrying her out the exit door.

To my surprise, she received those words as a starving man would greet an offer of bread.

"Help me up, Sheila. Help me sit up."

I put my arm under her back. She held onto the bed rail, and together we managed to get her into a sitting position. Then I propped a couple of pillows behind her to support her diminished weight.

"Get a piece of paper and a pen," she said. "And bring all my jewelry."

I ran downstairs and grabbed a piece of paper from the pad that William keeps by the phone. I picked up his pen and took two boxes of jewelry out of the drawers in the guest room where Eleanor keeps many of her things.

When I returned to her room, Eleanor's first words were, "Thank you. Thank you for asking."

"Mom, I hated to ask that, but I know that William and Barry can't bear to talk about this. Yet I want things to be the way you want them to be."

"Write it all down for me, will you?" Eleanor asked.

I picked up the pen.

"Pastor Paulwyn Boliek has already agreed to give the eulogy," she began. "And I want you to sing."

"Oh, Mom! I don't know if I'll be able to."

"Yes, you will. God will give you strength. And I want you to talk. You know that I don't want to die, but I'm not afraid of dying, and I know where I'm going. I would be thrilled to see all my friends and family at my funeral, but I would be more thrilled if I see them all again in heaven. You need to tell everyone who comes to the service everything that God did for me in my life by being part of Women of Faith. And then I want you to sing "How Great Thou Art.""

"All right, Mom . . . I'll do that."

"Now, I want to be buried in the outfit I wore to your wedding. I look good in that." We both smiled for a moment at the irony in those words.

"What about your jewelry, Mom?"

We picked out pieces of her jewelry for each one of the Women of Faith speakers and Mary and Lana.

"When you give these to them," she said, "tell them it's because they brought Christ to me."

"I will," I said, knowing how much that would mean to them.

"Oh yes, now find me the gold beads."

"What gold beads?" I asked. I was familiar with all of Eleanor's "good jewelry," because Barry and I had bought much of it for her, and there were no gold beads.

"The ones that slide on the chain," she said.

I rummaged through the two boxes and finally held up tarnished beads that must have cost less than twenty dollars. "Are these the ones?"

"Yes!" she said with a delight in her voice that I had not heard in a long time. She took them in her hands and examined each bead as if it were a precious stone. "I want to be buried with these on."

"Why, Mom?"

"Look at them!" she replied as she handed the gold necklace to me.

At first I didn't see anything unusual, and then I saw a dent on one particular bead. Tiny teeth marks. As I looked more closely, I saw them on almost every bead. I remembered how Christian loved to sit in his car seat beside his nana and chew her beads.

"Promise me you'll put them on me before the viewing."

"I promise, Mom," I answered with tears running down my face.

"And I want them in the casket with me, close to my heart." Then Eleanor took off her diamond ring. "What will I do with this?" she asked. "Would you like it, Sheila?"

"I'd love it, Mom. But I have a better idea. Why don't I keep it for Christian? When he meets the right girl, I'll give it to her as a gift from you."

A sob caught in her throat. I waited a moment, then I pulled down one side of the bed rails and lay down beside her and took her hand. We were quiet for a while. Then I turned to look at her, and tears were running down her face too.

"I don't want Christian to forget me," she said again, sobbing, using up strength she could ill afford.

"Mom, he won't forget you! You are part of the tapestry of his early life." I took her in my arms as if she were a child and rocked her for a while. I had no idea if I had just lied to a dying woman. Will a two-and-a-half-year-old child remember? I don't know. Even if it weren't true, I would have said the same thing.

Then together we sang what we believed and couldn't see:

> *All people that on earth do dwell,*
> *Sing to the Lord with cheerful voice;*
> *Him serve with fear, His praise forthtell,*
> *Come ye before Him and rejoice.*
>
> *The Lord, ye know, is God indeed;*
> *Without our aid He did us make;*
> *We are His flock, He doth us feed,*
> *And for His sheep He doth us take.*
>
> *O enter then His gates with praise,*
> *Approach with joy His courts unto;*
> *Praise, laud, and bless His name always,*
> *For it is seemly so to do.*
>
> *For why? the Lord our God is good,*
> *His mercy is forever sure:*
> *His truth at all times firmly stood,*
> *And shall from age to age endure.*
>
> *Praise God, from whom all blessings flow;*
> *Praise Him, all creatures here below;*
> *Praise Him above, ye heav'nly host;*
> *Praise Father, Son, and Holy Ghost.*[9]

The Piano

Have mercy on me, O God, have mercy on me,
*   for in you my soul takes refuge.*
I will take refuge in the shadow of your wings
*   until the disaster has passed.*

PSALM 57:1 NIV

Barry and I wanted to give a gift to Martin Luther Lutheran Church, where Eleanor had been a member for most of her life. The staff had been so kind to us all during this painful time, particularly Terry Doucette, one of the nurses who volunteered some hours at church and had come to see us every day. Christian loved her. She had brought him a stuffed animal from his favorite movie, *A Bug's Life*. (She is now his friend for life!) Terry went so far beyond anything you could expect, it was as if she were family. I saw the way she held William up, and I loved her for that too.

A week before Eleanor died, Barry and I asked her, "Is there anything special we could give to the church that would mean a lot to you?"

"Something to do with music," she answered immediately.

We called Mary Nell Whittaker, who serves on the church council, and asked her if they needed anything in the area of music.

"I don't know what kind of budget you are thinking of," she said, "but we sure do need a new piano."

I talked to Mom, and she thought that would be wonderful. Barry got catalogs with pictures of various pianos and showed them to her. She picked out a beautiful walnut baby grand. We contacted Kawai, the company who made this particular piano, and asked if it was available. The representative wasn't sure if there was even one in America at this time, but he said he'd try to find one.

That was a week before Eleanor died. The piano arrived the day she died, and the first time it was used to accompany a singer was when I sang "How Great Thou Art" at her funeral.

> *Then sings my soul,*
> *My Savior God, to Thee;*
> *How great Thou art,*
> *How great Thou art!* [10]

Eleanor's Favorite Hymn

A mighty fortress is our God,
A bulwark never failing;
Our helper He amid the flood
Of mortal ills prevailing.
For still our ancient foe
Doth seek to work us woe—
His craft and pow'r are great,
And, armed with cruel hate,
On earth is not his equal.

Did we in our own strength confide,
Our striving would be losing,
Were not the right man on our side,
The man of God's own choosing.
Dost ask who that may be?
Christ Jesus, it is He—
Lord Sabaoth, His name,
From age to age the same,
And He must win the battle.

And tho' this world, with devils filled,
Should threaten to undo us,
We will not fear, for God hath willed
His truth to triumph thru us.
The prince of darkness grim,
We tremble not for him—
His rage we can endure,
For lo, his doom is sure:
One little word shall fell him.

That word above all earthly pow'rs,
No thanks to them, abideth;
The Spirit and the gifts are ours
Thru Him who with us sideth.
Let good and kindred go,
This mortal life also—
The body they may kill;
God's truth abideth still,
His kingdom is forever.[11]

Good-byes

May our Lord Jesus Christ himself and God our Father,
who loved us and by his grace gave us eternal encourage-
ment and good hope, encourage your hearts and strengthen
you in every good deed and word.

2 THESSALONIANS 2:16–17 NIV

*I*t was early the morning of Monday, May 3. We all stood around Eleanor's bed. William was holding one hand and Barry the other. Christian was fast asleep in his crib downstairs.

"I know it's my time," she said. "I want to say something to each of you."

"Don't talk like that, Mom," Barry said.

"I want to," Eleanor replied. She turned to look at William. "William, you have been a good husband to me for forty-seven years. Not many men would have nursed me the way you have. I know I can be difficult at times."

"Not you, Mama!" William said with a wink.

She smiled.

"Barry. I'm not worried about you. You've been a wonderful son. You're a great husband and a fine daddy. You take care of that little boy and don't let him forget his nana."

"I won't, Mom," Barry replied with tears coursing down his cheeks. "I love you, Mom."

"I love you, too, Barry. I'm proud of you."

Then she turned to look at me. She let go of William and Barry's hands and took my face between her hands, holding it softly.

"Sheila!" She didn't say anything more for a few moments, but tears were running down her cheeks. Finally she spoke. "You have been a good daughter-in-law to me. Now you are my daughter."

I could say nothing in reply to such an honor. This was something only God could have done. I kissed her in gratitude and humility.

"We'll say good-bye now," she said.

"Do you think you are going to die tonight?" I asked.

"It's soon," she said.

"Then I'm canceling my appearance at the Kansas City Women of Faith Conference this weekend."

"Absolutely not!" she said. "You go and tell those women that God loves them. I'll be all right."

I didn't know what to do.

A while later William and Barry and I sat around the breakfast table.

"I know she wants you to go," William said. "She told me that. I'm sure she'll be here when you get back."

Three days later Barry, Christian, and I flew to Kansas City. We called as soon as we got to our hotel.

"She seems a little stronger," William said.

I was so relieved. I had asked God if I could be with her when she died; I so wanted to hand her to the Lord.

We got up at 4:00 A.M. the Sunday after the conference and

headed to the airport to catch the first flight. Once we had checked in, Barry said, "I think I'll call my dad."

"It's kind of early, babe. He might be asleep." We had hired a full-time nurse to be there when we were gone so that William could rest a little.

As Barry went to the bank of phones across from the gate, I took Christian to the bathroom to change his diaper. When we came back Barry was walking toward me. Before he said a word I knew she was gone; she had died the night before, Saturday, May 8.

We flew to Charleston on the first flight. As we were nearing the city, I tried to explain to Christian that Nana was with Jesus now, but he made no comment. William was there to pick us up, and Christian ran to hug him, not thinking anything was different. We drove to the house not saying much.

When we got inside Christian said, "Where is Nana?"

"Nana is with Jesus, darling. Remember, Mommy told you that on the plane."

"Oh yes," he said, "I forgot." He started to look through his little suitcase.

"What are you doing, little lamb?" I asked.

"I'm looking for my good shoes so that we can go and visit Nana and Jesus."

"Not today, darling," I said. I tried to explain to him that we couldn't go where Jesus and Nana were. Then he asked to go up to her room. I went with him. Her body was no longer there, but the white hospital bed was. He walked around the stark bed, and then said, "Nana's with Jesus."

"Yes, darling, Nana's with Jesus."

William came up and took Christian downstairs to have a snack, but I stayed in the room. Everything was the way it was before we left. The foot lotion was still sitting on the bedside table. I could smell the aroma of the therapy spray I had used on her forehead when she felt hot. There was the plastic cup with a straw and a little ginger ale still left in it. A bottle of liquid morphine, such a drastic friend, stood on the table by the bathroom, out of Christian's reach. The cassette player was at the foot of the bed. I pressed play and "Come Rest a While" came on. I lay on the bed and wept.

Later when the man came to dismantle the hospital bed and take it away, Christian said, "I want to watch them take Nana's bed down."

I had no idea what was going on in his mind. He and I just sat there on the carpet, leaning against the bedroom wall as we watched the men take the bed apart. Then, when they were carrying the bed away, Christian said to them, "Nana doesn't need the bed anymore because Nana's with Jesus."

One of the men smiled and said, "That's the best place to be, buddy."

I have no idea how much a two-and-a-half-year-old child can understand, but I do know that Christian is a very sensitive little boy. One time we had to get rid of one of his teddy bears because he thought the bear looked too sad. All I can do is watch him and love him and keep photos of Eleanor around.

I won't forget my promise, Mom.

Part Three

The Homecoming

Precious in the sight of the LORD
Is the death of His saints.

PSALM 116:15 NKJV

Treasures of Heaven

Come home, you weary traveler,
Come home, and be with Me.
Come bring to Me your shattered dreams
And lay them at My feet.
I will lead you into freedom now.
I will light the road ahead.
So come, take this hand I'm holding out
And suffer no regret.

All the treasures of heaven I will give to you,
For the chains that would bind you are broken in two.
All I ask is you love Me with all that you are.
And I promise the treasures of heaven will be yours.

Lay down those broken promises.
Bring Me your broken heart.
Lay down the years of trying hard
To make it on your own.
I have loved you with a perfect love.
I am here, so run to Me.
You are more to Me than precious stones.
Oh, child, now don't you see?[12]

The Viewing

Quiet now, so still.
Like a china doll, carefully kept, treasured, safe.
The tiny lines of pain around your eyes erased,
        smoothed by God's hand.
Quiet now, so still.

The actual viewing was a traumatic experience for me. For Barry it was devastating. Even though you know your mom is dying, and even though you are given some time to prepare with a disease like cancer, you are never ready to see your mother lying in a casket—so still, so absent.

I had never seen a dead body in my life, and like a child I was terrified to look. In Scotland when you die, you are sealed in a casket. There is no embalming or viewing at all.

An hour before the viewing was to start, Barry and I went down with William to make sure everything was the way Eleanor had wanted it. When Barry first saw his mom, he cried out in pain. I had never seen him in that kind of agony, and it broke my heart.

Finally I walked up to the casket. Eleanor had asked me to check that her jewelry was there and her makeup was the way she liked it. As I stood beside her casket, it was very clear to me that she was not there.

But she looked so beautiful and so peaceful. I put her favorite picture of her and Christian, hugging each other and smiling, into the casket. Her earrings were on crooked, so I reached out to fix them, and my hand brushed against her cold, smooth face. It was like an electric shock to touch that cheek again, the one I had stroked so often. I smiled as I saw the little gold beads on top

of the neckline of her dress, every tooth mark showing.

Barry was so distraught. At that moment I realized that our close friends are gifts of mercy and grace. Mary Graham, who has become like a big sister to Barry, was due to leave for Africa the day after the funeral. Yet the minute she heard that Eleanor had died, she said, "I will be there with you." She and Ney Bailey, two of the women we treasure most in the world, walked every last step with us. Now Mary stood at the casket beside Barry and me, at times holding him up.

One of Eleanor's fears was that no one would come to her funeral, since she considered herself to be difficult at times. But the viewing was packed with friends and flowers. Flowers from Luci Swindoll, Barbara Johnson, Thelma Wells, Marilyn Meberg, Patsy Clairmont, Joni Eareckson Tada, all these women of God whom she had met in the last two years of her life. They had been rivers of mercy and grace to her in a way that she had never before experienced. A lovely arrangement from Steve Arterburn, the head of Women of Faith and a dear friend. A beautiful heart-shaped wreath from Eleanor's sisters. Flowers from my mom and sister and brother-in-law. Flowers from neighbors and church friends.

It was overwhelming. Even at the viewing there was sorrow in saying good-bye, and joy in knowing how thrilled Eleanor would have been if she could have seen how packed that place was! As I think about that moment, I always remember what Joni Eareckson Tada's card said: "The setting is broken, but the diamond is safe."

Much of the rest of that evening is a blur to me now. So many people filed past the casket. I recognized some faces, but many were strangers to me. After about an hour some of Barry's old school friends came by. It was such a visible relief for him to move over to the corner of the room to talk to them. I stayed beside Eleanor. I knew she wasn't there, but she looked so vulnerable. I felt as if I wanted to protect her.

Then it was over, and we went home. We sat up for a while, talking about the evening, saying how beautiful she looked, how proud she would have been. Now she was home free.

"Pop?" I asked. "What was her last hour like?"

"She wasn't in any pain. She looked like a little girl," he said, looking off at a picture of the two of them that hung on the wall. "She said Barry's name once, then she picked up her favorite picture of Christian and you, laid it on her heart, and died."

"So, I was there, Pop?"

"You were there, darling."

God had answered my prayer.

I said to Barry and William, "Oh, by the way, I want to keep Mom's doll collection."

The resting place

The Funeral

Under a Southern tree,
Gentled by moss and by time,
Tenderly shaded,
It's quiet and still.
Rest now, sweet friend of mine.

As for man, his days are like grass,
    he flourishes like a flower of the field;
the wind blows over it and it is gone,
    and its place remembers it no more.
But from everlasting to everlasting
    the LORD's love is with those who fear him,
    and his righteousness with their children's children.

PSALM 103:15–17 NIV

On Tuesday, May 11, I had to be at Martin Luther Lutheran Church at 9:00 A.M. to rehearse with the pianist. I couldn't believe the piano had arrived on time. The sound was magnificent! I looked at the beautiful flowers everywhere and knew Eleanor would approve. She was a great floral arranger—she always said my flowers looked more abandoned than arranged! She was right.

Then I drove back to the house for William and Barry. Pastor Paulwyn Boliek had arrived, and he seemed to be a kind man. He hugged William and Barry. He hugged me and high-fived Christian.

Soon the limousine pulled up in front of the Pfaehlers's gray house. For a moment I wanted to laugh. It was the same limo that had taken us to the wedding!

Once we arrived at the church, William, Barry, Mary, and I went in the back door to wait for the casket; from this entry area we could see the sanctuary. The church was packed; people were even sitting in the choir loft. I saw Emily Schroeder there and noticed her admiring the flower arrangements. We were so pleased to see everyone, but when they brought in the casket, it was too much for Barry. I held him up as we followed it to the front of the sanctuary.

Barry wasn't sure if the minister would say something sweet about Eleanor or if he would challenge people spiritually. Reverend Boliek did both, and Barry and I will always remember his explanation of a passage from Romans 14:8 NKJV: "For if we live, we live to the Lord; and if we die, we die to the Lord. Therefore, whether we live or die, we are the Lord's."

Without knowing it, Reverend Boliek expressed much of what the Lord had been teaching me during my walk with Eleanor in her last days. Coincidence? I don't think so.

Reverend Boliek began by saying, "When my children first studied possessives in public school, we were living right here on James Island. One of the things I have always loved about this area is the marvelous twist to the English language that a

Charleston accent gives. Eleanor and Bubsie (a pet name given to William by his mom) were both perfect examples of that. Charlestonians often add the word *own* following a possessive for emphasis. They say, 'That's Mama's own book,' or 'That's John's own car.'

"I'm not certain that is correct grammar, but it is interesting that St. Paul used it in his first epistle. He explained that the church was 'a chosen generation, God's own special people.' A double possessive.

"That's what St. Paul is saying to the Romans and to us. Whether we live or whether we die—no matter what happens to us—we are the Lord's. We belong to Him; we are in His care.

"It is a wonderful thing to belong to someone and to have someone belong to you. That's what life is all about."

Sitting in the front pew of that paneled sanctuary, I thought, *Yes, Lord. That's just what You've been teaching me.*

Reverend Boliek went on to explain. "What makes us human is not so much that we are rational beings, but that we are relational beings. We are related to each other by blood or marriage or friendship or faith. And even more wonderful, we are related to God Himself. *'We are the Lord's.'*

"Eleanor understood all of this. She was a mother who had taught possessives to Barry. And she was also a child of God. She knew about living and dying and living again."

Pastor Boliek concluded his sermon with these words, "The gospel for today, the good news for us, is that we belong to this same Lord . . . so that whether we live or whether we die, we and Eleanor are the Lord's."

Then it was time for me. I walked toward the casket and turned to face everyone. I don't remember much of what I said. I remember joking about the fact that William and Eleanor had been married for forty-seven years and lived in the same house, and Barry and I had been married five years and lived in six homes! I know I thanked everyone for coming. I told them that Eleanor was not afraid to die.

"She was so at peace," I said. "She found in her dying what she had been looking for in her living: a close, intimate relationship with Jesus Christ and with those she loved. Eleanor and I were both changed by the experience of her dying, even though it wasn't what either of us had asked for."

Then I quoted Eleanor, "You know that I don't want to die, but I'm not afraid of dying and I know where I'm going. I would be thrilled to see all my friends and family at my funeral, but I would be more thrilled if I see them all again in heaven. You need to tell everyone who comes to the service everything that God did for me in my life."

Finally I sang "How Great Thou Art," as I had promised. I sang with a joy I didn't know I had at that time. But in my mind's eye I could see Eleanor, free at last, singing around the throne of grace.

I didn't know what would happen at the cemetery. We were given the choice to leave after the short interment service, but Barry wanted us to stay until the final moment. We sat as the workers lowered the casket and shoveled every piece of dirt back into the ground. Barry wouldn't leave his mother until it was all over.

Later that day, once everyone had left the house, we went back to the cemetery with Mary Graham and Patsy Clairmont. We took Christian. Barry, William, and I sat under the shade of the tree that sheltered Eleanor's grave.

"Pretty flowers, Mommy!" Christian said as he danced round and round the tree. "I like this park."

Later that night, when all the trauma of the viewing and the burial was over and William and Barry were asleep, I lay on the bathroom floor for an hour and sobbed. I was aching for Eleanor, for William, for Barry, for Christian, for me, for all of us—for the frailty of this human life, which is never what it could have been.

Once we knew Eleanor was dying, I had thought, *Barry, you don't realize how much you are going to miss your mom, even though she drives you crazy at times. You think you are all grown up, and you are married now, and you're a dad. But you're going to miss your mom.*

With William I thought, *You have had forty-seven years, and you've had a long time of nursing her through her illness. In some ways it's a relief to be over those last days, but there are going to be moments when it's going to be so painful for you.*

What I hadn't taken into account was how Eleanor's death was going to grieve my heart; I, too, was going to miss her. That was almost a sweet pain. At times in the past I had thought, *You are so difficult, Eleanor.* Yet after our journey together in the past months, I had lost a dear, dear friend. That moment by myself, when everyone else was settled in bed, gave me time to do my own private grieving.

> *You are precious beyond measure.*
> *You're a river running free*
> *To the lives of Adam's broken ones,*

For Your river has saved me.

If I live to be a hundred years, I'll never understand,

King of kings,

Lord of lords,

All the grace that's in Your hands.

My Three Boys!

God sets the solitary in families.

PSALM 68:6 NKJV

Barry and I always knew that when his mom died we would want William to come live with us. What I didn't know was how much I'd love it. We are a new nuclear family. Four of us. I'm usually up by 6:00 A.M., as I like some time to write, study, and be quiet before Christian wakes up. I make coffee and fetch the paper for William. He gets up about 7:00, and we split the paper and read bits of it to each other. We all travel together and help each other. I love my life. I am a blessed woman.

A month after the funeral, William decided to go back to Charleston for a week to tidy up some loose ends.

"Do you want me to go with you?" Barry asked.

"No," he said. "I want to do this by myself."

"Call me when you get there, Pop," I said. "Just so I know you arrived safely."

That evening, when Christian was asleep, I said to Barry, "What if Pop likes being by himself and doesn't want to live with us? I would miss him so much."

"We'll have to wait and see, babe . . . That would be his choice."

That night William called to say he'd made it home safely.

"Was it hard walking into the house alone?" I asked.

"Yes," he replied. "I cried for a while."

"That's good, Pop, you need to cry."

"Love you past heaven!" he said as he hung up with his favorite farewell.

I'd always been curious about this remark, so I asked Barry, "What on earth does that mean? There is no place 'past heaven.'"

Barry laughed. "That's just my dad. He just means forever and ever."

The next morning William called again. "Do you miss me?" he asked tentatively.

"Are you kidding!" I said. "We all miss you."

"Then I'm coming home!"

I was so happy, I made pancakes!

Even though we began adjusting to our new life without Eleanor, the next Women of Faith Conference, which was June 11, a month after her death, was hard. It was the first time I had to speak to this large gathering, over fifteen thousand women, seated in the round in the huge Detroit arena. I didn't know how I was going to get through it.

About an hour before the conference began, Marilyn Meberg said, "You won't believe what I've done." She and I had gone to the Escada store in New York, which had a huge final sale, and we had managed to find two suits each.

"I brought both the suit jackets," she said, "but I don't have the pants! I'm going to have to go on stage tonight with what I wore flying here!" She was embarrassed to be in her jeans, but she looked great to me.

Marilyn decided to make a big joke about her attire when all six of us spoke for two minutes on Friday night, before I gave my main talk. When she got up, she told the audience what she had done, and said, "I hope you like what I'm wearing because I will be wearing it till Sunday."

Everyone laughed and we moved on.

Halfway through my talk that night I came to the part where I talk about Eleanor. I looked at the vast crowd in the arena; our stage is always in the center, so we can see the entire amphitheater. My eyes went up to the top tier, and there was William, standing under one of the exit signs, all by himself, his silhouette outlined against the light. All alone.

I had to stop for a moment. I couldn't go on. I suddenly felt so sad for him to have lost his partner of forty-seven years. Tears began to run down my face. I turned to my friends sitting on what we call "the porch." (All six speakers stay in the arena for the entire conference so we can support each other.)

"Marilyn, would you give me a tissue?" I asked.

She immediately grabbed one from the box on the porch and came on stage. As she handed the Kleenex to me and turned to leave, I said, "Nice outfit, Marilyn!"

All fifteen thousand women broke into laughter.

It was just the moment of relief I needed, an unexpected grace in the midst of a broken dream.

The grass withers, the flower fades
Because the breath of the LORD blows upon it;
Surely the people are grass.
The grass withers, the flower fades,
But the word of our God stands forever . . .

He will feed His flock like a shepherd;
He will gather the lambs with His arm,
And carry them in His bosom,
And gently lead those who are with young.

ISAIAH 40:7–8, 11 NKJV

$\mathcal{S}$heila and Christian in Scotland

A Final Word to the Reader

I began this book by saying that Eleanor found in her dying what she had been looking for in her living and that I got "over myself" enough to see beyond the stuff that doesn't matter to love my mother-in-law, my sister in Christ. I told you that the events that happened in the last few weeks of her life made me realize I could try to write this, because in the end Eleanor trusted me in her most vulnerable, weak moments.

No words can express my gratitude to God for plunging Eleanor and me into His river of mercy. We could have lived our whole lives and never reached out to each other—and we would have missed so much. Each of us longs for an intimate relationship, but we are most afraid of it because we will be seen in all our colors—some pretty, some dark and ugly.

Yet I am finding out that when we take that risk to be known and loved, the very process gives us an opportunity to change. Eleanor was gifted with peace in the midst of pain. I see now that Christ does not always remove the pain. He meets us in the middle of it and walks with us to the other side. There are too many mysteries here for me to grasp, but I do know this: it is easy to love those who are like us, but we are changed by loving those who are not.

A Letter to Eleanor

October 8, 1999

Dear Eleanor,

It's been five months now. I can hardly believe it, and yet sometimes it seems much longer. I'm not sure why I'm writing this letter. I don't have heaven's zip code, and you're way too busy singing to read your mail, but I wanted to imagine that I could let you take a peek at our lives, now that you are gone.

You looked so beautiful lying in your casket. Barry cried. He said it was how he remembered you when he was a little boy. I joked with the guy who does the embalming and asked if he had any free samples. (As you can see, my humor has not improved!)

William didn't cry until two nights after the funeral. I put on a videotape of you and Christian when he was about a year old. Christian saw you and cried out with joy, "There's Nana!" He ran to the television set and threw his arms around it, and then kissed your face on the screen. William went into the dining room and wept. He needed to.

So now we are four. It's me and your boys! William moved to Nashville to live with us right after the funeral. We love having him here. He actually behaved for three weeks; he did not rearrange one cabinet. But the pressure was too great, so now everything is in a different place.

I don't mind anymore. Your dying taught me that. I think of all the time you and I wasted fretting over stupid stuff. Now the four of us just try to love each other. I wish I'd loved you better, Eleanor, but I'm so grateful we finally found each other in God's arms.

William seems happy. He never sits down for two minutes. You know how he is! Every once in a while, though, I'll find him sitting alone in the kitchen with a certain look in his eyes, and I know he is thinking about you and missing you. We all do. I have your photographs all over the house so that you can live with us too.

Sometimes when Christian passes them, he stops, picks one up, and says, "Hello, Nana!"

Barry keeps a bottle of your favorite cologne in our bathroom. Man, it sure stinks! I wish I'd bought you something different. Barry misses you every day. Every day. Every single day. You were loved more than you understood.

Christian is getting so big. I can't believe he's almost three. It's so fun for him to have his papa living with us. I have to share rocking him to sleep now. Some weeks I only get three nights! Watching you die taught me to share.

I tell our story now at Women of Faith. You would not believe how many women line up for two hours to thank us and to say they are going home after the conference to love one another better. You left a lot behind. I think of a passage in an Oswald Chambers book Patsy Clairmont gave me. He talks about our suffering not being for us alone. I see that now. I see how God redeems our pain, not only in our lives but also in the lives of others. I guess you and I got to be the "before" picture! I'm more grateful than I can say that we got to taste a little of the "after."

Now you are home! Oh, I wish you could send me photographs! Have you met my dad? He's the handsome one with the great voice. Does everything make sense to you now, or are you so blown away by the Lamb that you forget the small stuff? So many questions.

I find myself thinking of you often. I'll be in a mall in one of the cities in our travels, and I'll see something in a store and think, *Eleanor would have liked that!* Once I almost bought a pair of shoes for you. I forgot you weren't still with us.

I have to go now. Christian, Barry, and William will be back any moment. They have been off doing a "guy thing" that involves hamburgers.

I'm so glad you were in my life for a while. I am a better woman because of you. I am committed to gleaning lessons for my living from your dying: I stop more now. I listen more. I celebrate more. I "get over" myself most of the time and let the little things go. I want to be a woman of faith—not just in a conference but in my life.

I'll take good care of your boys. We'll all be home soon, and then this life with all its joys and heartaches will be nothing more than a faint whisper. Good-bye, Eleanor . . . and thank you!

Your loving daughter,

Sheila

Notes

1. "Saving Grace." Written by Sheila Walsh, John Hartley, and Gary Sadler. © 2000 Integrity's Hosanna! Music/ASCAP and Worshiptogether.com Songs (adm. by EMI Christian Music Publishing). All rights reserved. International copyright secured. Used by permission.

2. Sonnet by William Shakespeare, first published in 1609. Source: *The Oxford Anthology of English Literature*, Vol. 1, Frank Kermode and John Hollander, eds. (New York: Oxford University Press, 1973).

3. "The Race." Words by Sheila Walsh. © 1998 Little Pilgrim Music. Used by permission.

4. "Blue Waters." Written by Sheila Walsh, John Hartley, and Margaret Becker. © 2000 Integrity's Hosanna! Music/ASCAP and Worshiptogether.com Songs and His Eye Music (adm. by EMI Christian Music Publishing) and Maggie Bee's Music (adm. by EMI Christian Music Publishing).

5. "Let His Love Flow Down." Words by Sheila Walsh. © 1998 Little Pilgrim Music. Used by permission.

6. "The Book of Joy and Sorrow." Words by Sheila Walsh. © 1998 Little Pilgrim Music. Used by permission.

7. "Joy." Words by Sheila Walsh. © 1998 Little Pilgrim Music. Used by permission.

8. "Great Is Thy Faithfulness." Words by Thomas O. Chisholm (1866–1960).

9. "All People That on Earth Do Dwell." Stanzas 1–4 paraphrase of William Kethe, circa 1561. Stanza 5 by Thomas Ken (1637–1711).

10. "How Great Thou Art." © Copyright 1953 Stuart K. Hine. Assigned to MANNA MUSIC, INC., 35255 Brooten Road, Pacific City, OR 97135. Renewed 1981. All rights reserved. Used by permission.

11. "A Mighty Fortress Is Our God." Words by Martin Luther (1483–1546); translated by Frederick H. Hedge (1805–1890).

12. "Treasures of Heaven." Words by Sheila Walsh. © 1998 Little Pilgrim Music. Used by permission.

About the Author

SHEILA WALSH is a powerful Christian communicator who is a unique combination of singer, songwriter, author, speaker, and television talk-show host. She is a featured speaker at the nationwide Women of Faith Conferences and has just released her new Celtic album, *Blue Waters*, with Integrity Music. Former cohost of *The 700 Club* and host of her own show, *Heart to Heart with Sheila Walsh*, on the Family Channel, she is the author of *Honestly* and *Life Is Tough But God Is Faithful*.

Sheila and her husband, Barry, and their son, Christian, live in Franklin, Tennessee.

For information on Sheila's tour schedule and her online bookstore, see her Web site at www.sheilawalsh.com.

Life Is Tough But God Is Faithful

If God loves me, why did my child die?
If life is supposed to be so wonderful, why do I feel so bad?
If God hears my prayers, why am I still single?
If God is in control of the world, why is life so hard?

Sheila Walsh hears questions like these wherever she goes. In her own life journey, she has struggled with difficult questions—and found some answers. Not easy, pat answers, but real-life, lived-out-in-the-flesh answers that can help you find meaning and purpose in spite of pain and suffering. In *Life Is Tough But God Is Faithful*, Sheila looks at eight crucial turning points that can help you rediscover God's love and forgiveness. She offers encouraging insight into God's presence in the midst of our questions and struggles—and highlights positive choices you can make, no matter what your circumstances.

0-7852-6914-2 • Hardcover • 224 pages

sheila walsh

B L U E
Waters

Available in CD and cassette.
To locate the Christian bookstore
nearest you, call **1-800-991-7747**.

INTEGRITY
MUSIC.

www.integritymusic.com
© 2000 Integrity Incorporated